READER BONUS!

Dear Reader,

As a thank you for your support, Action Takers Publishing would like to offer you a special reader bonus: a free download of our course, "How to Write, Publish, Market & Monetize Your Book the Fast, Fun & Easy Way." This comprehensive course is designed to provide you with the tools and knowledge you need to bring your book to life and turn it into a successful venture.

The course typically **retails for $499**, but as a valued reader, you can access it for free. To claim your free download, simply follow this link <u>ActionTakersPublishing.com/workshops</u> - use the discount code "coursefree" to get a 100% discount and start writing your book today.

If we are still giving away this course by the time you're reading this book, head straight over to your computer and start the course now. It's absolutely free.

READER BONUS!

<u>ActionTakersPublishing.com/workshops</u>
discount code "coursefree"

FINDING
YOUR PURPOSE

Email: lynda@actiontakerspublishing.com

Website: www.actiontakerspublishing.com

ISBN # (paperback) 978-1-956665-44-4

ISBN # (Kindle) 978-1-956665-45-1

Published by Action Takers Publishing™

Table of Contents

Walking into a room with an open mind enables opportunities to jump in.
~Lynda Sunshine West

FOREWORD

Jeff Hoffman

When I reflect on the incredible journey of life, I'm reminded of the profound impact that purpose can have. It's a force that can transform the ordinary into the extraordinary and turn dreams into reality.

In *"Finding Your Purpose: Living on Purpose Rather than on Accident,"* you are about to embark on a remarkable journey alongside a community of inspiring authors. These individuals have opened their hearts and shared their personal odysseys in pursuit of one of life's most profound questions: "What is my purpose?"

Throughout my own entrepreneurial journey, I've come to understand that purpose is not just a destination but a guiding star, a relentless pursuit that propels us forward. It's the force that empowers us to create, innovate, and, above all, make a difference.

The stories you will encounter in this book are not mere tales; they are blueprints for discovering your own purpose. Each author has ventured into the depths of self-discovery, navigated the uncertainties of life, and emerged stronger, wiser, and driven by a sense of purpose.

As a serial entrepreneur who helped launch multiple startups (Priceline.com/Booking.com, uBid.com, and others) and the Founder and CEO of World Youth Horizons (a nonprofit organization that provides support to youth around the world by providing food, shelter, education, and experiences to help improve their economic conditions and to encourage youth to expand their horizons), I've witnessed how purpose can shape industries, disrupt norms, and redefine success. But it's not just about business; it's about the profound impact we can have on the world when we align our actions with our purpose.

"Finding Your Purpose" is more than a book; it's a movement. It's a call to action for all of us to live our lives with intention, to embrace the journey of self-discovery, and to make our mark on the world. It's a reminder that we have the power to inspire change, to alter trajectories, and to illuminate the path for others.

So, as you turn these pages and immerse yourself in the stories of these incredible authors, I invite you to reflect on your own journey. What is your purpose? What legacy do you want to leave behind? And how can you, too, live "On Purpose" rather than on accident?

I commend each author for their courage, vulnerability, and commitment to sharing their stories. As you read this book, remember that your journey toward purpose is a profound one, and it's one that has the potential to change not only your life but the lives of countless others.

Let this book be your guide, your inspiration, and your catalyst for living a life of purpose, impact, and fulfillment. Together, we can light the way for a brighter, purpose-driven future.

Jeff Hoffman

Serial Entrepreneur, Priceline.com/Booking.com, uBid.com and more

Founder & President, World Youth Horizons

www.jeffhoffman.com

Introduction

Why do you do what you do?

What drives you?

What moves you into action?

Before you delve deeper into these pages, grab a pen and let your thoughts flow onto these very pages of the book. (For those who prefer to keep their books pristine, rest assured, we wholeheartedly encourage this creative act of jotting down your thoughts.)

Now that you have your answers, let's embark on a journey together.

Purpose, passion, and drive are the sacred sparks that ignite our actions.

Purpose, passion, and drive are the gentle yet relentless whispers that keep us going when we're tempted to surrender.

Purpose, passion, and drive are the guiding stars that help us navigate through the distractions of our fast-paced, action-filled world.

When you comprehend the WHY behind your actions and carry the blazing torch of passion and purpose, you become a force of unwavering determination, always aligned with your mission.

"Finding Your Purpose: Living 'On Purpose' Rather Than on Accident" was conceived from the author's personal odyssey in search of meaning, a quest to decipher her raison d'être, and identify those she's meant to serve. Once she unearthed her purpose, she realized that she had spent too many moments of her life merely existing "on accident."

Her conviction is this: when we discover our purpose, it's our job and duty to live the rest of our lives "on purpose," steering clear of the treacherous path of mere coincidence.

What is your purpose?

What actions are you taking to breathe life into your purpose?

Are you committed to the journey, ready to take each step with intention?

Within the pages of this book, you will find the kindling for inspiration and the fuel for motivation on your quest to uncover your purpose. Every author has traversed this path, and their stories are here to guide you in finding your own purpose, or perhaps to reignite the flame if you've already found it.

Welcome to *"Finding Your Purpose: Living 'On Purpose' Rather Than on Accident."* Let's embark on this transformative journey together.

Lynda Sunshine West and Sally Larkin Green

CHAPTER 1

How I Found My Purpose

Lynda Sunshine West

I dedicate this book to everyone who is searching for their purpose in life. Keep looking and you will find it.
Matthew 7:7: "Ask, and it shall be given you; seek, and ye shall find; knock, and it shall be opened unto you."

---

*"*I have no purpose, no value. Why am I here? Why is this planet here? What's this planet all about? Really, why … AM … I … here? I have zero value."

I screamed those words one day while stuck in traffic driving to my 49th job after working in the corporate world for 36 years. I "made it." I was working for a judge in the Ninth Circuit Court of Appeals. That was the penultimate. I should have been ecstatic with what I was doing. I was important. My job was important. I was valuable (so I thought).

I remember the day I was hired for that job. It was actually kind of odd. I applied (just like 85 other applicants). I was called in for an interview. I talked to the judge and his clerk (Randy) for about 15 minutes getting the formalities out of the way, when the judge asked me this question: "What are you passionate about?" I froze for what felt like an hour, staring into the ceiling wondering how I should answer. Should I say what I think he wants me to say or should I tell the truth and let the chips fall where they may?

"Well, I'm not passionate about the law. What I'm really passionate about is helping people who need help. I love putting on fundraising events. My husband and I have a band and we play for charity, donating 100% of the money we make to charities to help various causes."

Uh-oh. I blew it. I can't believe I said, "I'm not passionate about the law."

What was that all about? I was being interviewed to work for a judge in the court of appeals, a judge who had been practicing law for more than 55 years. Surely he wants a secretary who is passionate about the law.

We talked for another 10 minutes and then the clerk asked me to wait outside the door and he would walk me downstairs and out the building.

As I stood there waiting (wondering why I was waiting because I'm perfectly capable of walking to the elevator and making my way outside), I was filled with anguish. My stomach was in knots because of what I had said. I was mentally beating myself up. "I shouldn't have said that. That was so stupid to say. They'll never hire me." I was my own worst enemy at that time in my life and I did a great job of attacking myself.

Finally, Randy came out of the judge's chambers and, as we rode down the elevator to the first floor, it was completely silent. It was as if I were being walked down "The Green Mile" to my last breath. It was an incredibly awkward moment, me knowing I didn't get the job and having my "chaperone" walk me out the building.

The elevator doors opened and Randy, instead of saying goodbye and going back upstairs, walked out of the elevator with me. "What the heck is going on here? What a weirdo. Why is he following me? Just let me get out of here and go home to lick my wounds." My mind was racing.

"Lynda, the judge and I both like you a lot."

"Oh, no, here it comes. They've already decided they don't want me. Why couldn't he just send me a letter or email telling me I'm not the one," I thought.

"We'd like to offer you the position. I see that you requested the highest salary. We don't normally do this, but we are going to 'step you out' (government lingo for 'we're going to pay you the highest amount of money on the pay scale') because we want to make sure you accept the position."

I was in shock. Not only was I being offered the position, I was getting a $15,000 a year raise, too? Wow! I couldn't believe it.

The government doesn't move this fast EVER!

What's going on here?

I figured I'd go home and maybe hear back in two weeks or so.

"I'll take it. When can I start?," I squealed with pure joy.

"I have a question, though. When I said I'm not passionate about the law, I thought for sure that was a deal-breaker and that the judge wouldn't even consider me. Why did he hire me when I'm not passionate about the law?"

"Well, his previous secretary kept secrets from him and lied about a lot of things. He ended up firing her after only five months. Then, after she left, I was cleaning out her desk and found a lot of travel reimbursements that she never turned in for him. There were 85 applicants and only five were offered interviews – you are one of them. All of the other interviewees answered that question in a way that the judge and I knew they were trying to butter him up because they wanted the job. The judge is hiring you because you were honest. Plain and simple. You didn't try to tell him what he wanted to hear. He knows that if you were honest during your interview that you will be honest when working with him. Honesty is the most important thing to him. He has to know that he can trust you. Based on your response, he trusts your character to do the right thing."

I worked my way up the corporate ladder to land that job. I never once stepped on someone to climb the ladder. I was always honest and got in trouble sometimes for the things I did, but I always told the truth, admitted my mistakes, and took full blame when something was my fault. That integrity paid off in the end by getting hired for that very thing, honesty.

I was so excited when I got hired by the judge. I showed up to work, learned my job, and was damn good at it. I walked around town like I was someone. "I made it." Month after month, though, it got less and less glamorous, less and less challenging, and more and more boring.

That day when I was driving to work stuck in that same traffic I'd been stuck in for 36 years, I had a HUGE epiphany. "I hate my job" (again). But this time something was different. Instead of quitting, I decided this would be my last job and I would hold onto it until I figured out my next step (rather than jumping (like I had done the previous 36 years) without a plan).

When I got to work that day, there was a Facebook post from a woman named Liz. It said, "I'm a life coach. I took some time off and I'm getting back into it. I'm looking for five women who want to change their lives."

I didn't know what a life coach was or how it might help me, but I knew one thing: I wanted to change my life. So I took a chance and hired Liz.

That is the greatest gift I have ever given to myself, the gift of saying "yes" to me.

I worked with Liz for five glorious months. The amount of transformation that came while working with Liz was incredible. I started figuring out who I am and "why I'm here." It was a time of constant growth. I was looking deeply at myself. This deep reflection was necessary in order for me to make the shifts I made in my life.

Day after day I showed up to work excited about the transformation that was occurring. My transformation was fast and furious. After a short five months, I had changed so much that I was ready to jump out of the job and NO LONGER work for someone.

November 26, 2014, is the day my life started. That was my freedom day, the day I became an entrepreneur.

Life is hard. There are many ups and downs, twists and turns, backwards and forwards, failures and successes. It might actually be pretty boring if everything were pixies and rainbows, but perfection is something that many of us strive for.

As I was sitting in an airplane on my way to Hawaii with my Wheatie (my nickname for my husband), I decided to watch a movie with Jane Fonda, Lily Tomlin, Sally Field, Rita Moreno and Tom Brady, called 80 for Brady. What does this movie have to do with purpose? Everything.

Purpose comes in many forms. There are doctors saving lives, lawyers keeping the judicial system running, politicians doing whatever it is they do, preachers giving people guidance and hope, book publishers (like me) helping people share their stories with the world to make a greater impact on the planet, and then there's entertainers. The movie got me thinking about how every single one of us has a purpose.

As I watched the actors working their craft to bring laughter and tears to me, and watching the football players "playing" their game while bringing laughter, anger, joy and pain to their fans, it dawned on me that the rollercoaster of life lives within us and our purpose and passion is what drives us to do what we do.

Entertainers and athletes are highly paid and there's a reason, their purpose – to entertain. Entertainers bring joy to an otherwise humdrum life and, therefore, is a very special purpose.

I was always a quick-witted, funny person. I was a joker and knew how to make people laugh. My problem was that I had no idea they were laughing because of me. Nope. I was so self-conscious that I thought they were laughing at me. Because of my tremendous fear of judgment, I never got into stand-up comedy or acting. Looking back, I would have been really good at it. But that isn't my purpose.

I do love to entertain, but in a different capacity. I absolutely love what I do to help others tap into their stories to share them with the world to make a greater impact on the planet.

How did I get here? This is my journey to finding my purpose.

I spent the first 51 years of my life purposeless. I had drive and passion, but it was mostly fueled by my negative mindset. I wanted what others had, so I kept trying to get it, but I didn't know how.

You see, I ran away when I was five years old and was gone for a week. I just ran to the neighbor's house and was safe, but nobody came to get me. My mom knew where I was, but I didn't know she knew where I was.

Five is a very impressionable age and I'm told that our belief system is formed from birth to age seven, so I was ready to lock in my belief system. I became instilled with the belief that no one came to get me because they didn't love me and didn't want me around. That was my belief until I was 51 years old, the year I found my life coach (Liz).

After five months of working with Liz, I was armed with a set of tools and techniques to move me forward. My mind, heart, body, and soul were opened up to possibilities. I was starting to step into who I am meant to be.

The early morning of January 1, 2015, something inside of me broke loose. I had an earth-shattering epiphany. It was a split second that would shape my future. I experienced a realization that I was riddled with fear and that I allowed my fears to control my life. Wow! That awareness was huge.

Once we have awareness, we can effect change. I didn't know it at the time, but that was the single most important moment of my life.

I said (out loud to myself), "I have so many fears that are stopping me from living my life. I'm going to break through one fear every day this year."

That was not a New Year's resolution; it was a New Year's commitment.

365 days in a row I started every day the same way. It looked like this:

1. Wake up

2. Open eyes

3. Ask myself this question out loud, "What scares me?"

4. Stay in bed until the first fear pops into my head

5. Break through that fear THAT day

You can read about my fear-busting journey in my bestselling book, endorsed by motivational speaker Les Brown, "*The Year of Fears.*"

Breaking through those fears was life-altering. That year put me on the path to finding my purpose.

I no longer let fear fail me. Instead, I now embrace fear and live by my new motto, "*Do It BECAUSE You're Scared,*" the title of my most recently published book.

I learned a lot that year, but the greatest thing I learned was that 99% of the time we break through fears, we are either proud of ourselves, the results on the other side were better than we ever imagined, or a door was opened that we didn't even know was closed. On the other side of fear are endless possibilities and opportunities.

Ask yourself this question when you're experiencing fear, "Why am I depriving myself of the opportunities that await me on the other side?" and then say, "I'm going to do it BECAUSE I'm scared."

Every fear you break through gets you one step closer to discovering your purpose. What's your purpose? What steps are you taking to get you closer to living the rest of your life "on purpose" rather than "on accident."

Lynda Sunshine West

She ran away at 5 years old and was gone an entire week, came home riddled with fears and, in turn, became a people-pleaser. At age 51, she decided to break through one fear every day for a year and, in doing so, she gained an exorbitant amount of confidence to share her story. Her mission is to empower 5 million women and men to write their stories to make a greater impact on the planet. Lynda Sunshine West is the Founder and CEO of Action Takers Publishing, a Bestseller Book Publishing Expert, Speaker, 36 Times #1 International Bestselling Author, Contributing Writer at Entrepreneur Magazine, Senior Level Executive Contributing Writer at Brainz Magazine, Executive Film Producer, and Red Carpet Interviewer.

Connect with Lynda Sunshine at

https://www.actiontakerspublishing.com

CHAPTER 2
Crossroads

Sally Larkin Green

---

*I dedicate this book to my husband, Billy, who has
encouraged me to find my purpose. To my friend and
mentor, Lynda Sunshine West, who motivates me to take
action and do things that scare me.*

Have you ever stood at a crossroads, wondering which path would lead you to a life of purpose and fulfillment? I've been there, too, standing paralyzed at life's many intersections, questioning the road signs, doubting the map, and even second-guessing my own desires. Purpose isn't something that's handed to you with your birth certificate, nor is it a secret formula that only a chosen few are privy to. Finding your purpose is a winding journey, often marked by dead ends, detours, and unexpected scenic routes that enrich your soul. It's a path that I've walked, stumbled, and sometimes even crawled, as I transformed from a person neglecting my own well-being into the self-care rockstar I am today.

Just a few years ago, I was overwhelmed by the multiple roles I juggled as a mom, wife, daughter and business owner. I was endlessly caught up in the current of responsibilities, with no time to question where the river was taking me. When the pandemic of 2020 hit, it was a wake-up call for me. It forced me to pause and reflect on my life. It wasn't until I took a leap of faith and invested in myself by joining a multi-author collaboration book that I felt the current shift within me. This seemingly small step was a turning point, a spark that ignited my quest to not just survive each day but to live it fully, joyfully, and with intention.

If you're reading this chapter, you're probably seeking answers to some of the same questions I had. "What is my purpose? How can I find it, and what do I need to do to get there?"

In the story that follows, I'll share the twists and turns of my journey, the revelations that guided me, and the tangible steps that can guide you, too. As a Christian and someone who's been through the grind, I'll dive into the role my faith has played, the incredible power of relationships, and the significance of simple yet mindful actions that can redirect your life's trajectory.

So, are you ready to step off the beaten path, to wander through uncharted territories of the self, and emerge with a life that doesn't just look good on paper, but feels phenomenal to your very core? Let's set forth on this exploration together.

Imagine life is a movie. The part where you're searching for your "why" is like that important scene with emotional music in the background. A few years ago, that was me. My days felt like they were on repeat—same tasks, same responsibilities, all in a loop. I had a job, took care of my family, and was part of my community. But something was missing. I felt like I was just floating through life without a clear direction.

It's a peculiar kind of loneliness, days filled with tasks that never seem to scratch the surface of what you truly desire. Nights staring at the ceiling, wondering if this is all there is to life. I tried filling the void with what I thought was missing: career achievements, social outings, and even weekend painting sessions that I loved so much. But those things, as fulfilling as they were, felt like temporary Band-Aids on a wound that required surgery.

And then came the game changer—the day I decided to invest in myself by joining a multi-author collaboration book. It was as if someone had thrown me a lifeline amidst a stormy sea of uncertainty. Little did I know that this seemingly insignificant step would serve as a pivot, turning me toward a journey that was as much about discovering myself as it was about impacting the lives of others.

In everyone's life, there are defining moments that act like signposts, nudging us toward our true north. For me, two pivotal events drastically altered the course of my journey, propelling me into a life imbued with purpose and fulfillment.

The first transformative moment was proclaiming myself as a self-care rockstar. The term may sound flashy, but the journey to earn it was anything but glamorous. It was born from years of neglecting my own well-being. I realized that taking care of myself wasn't an act of selfishness but one of necessity. And as I embraced self-love, I discovered that I could inspire others to do the same. My own transformation provided me with firsthand knowledge to help women empower themselves, cementing my sense of purpose even more.

The second was becoming part of a multi-author anthology book. This wasn't just a writing opportunity; it was my ticket to self-investment. I had spent years doing everything by the book—career, family, community—but had neglected the most important project: myself. Joining this anthology felt like a lifeline, offering a flicker of direction in a sea of monotony. It propelled me not just into the world of publishing but into a community of like-minded people I am now honored to call friends. It was like finding my tribe, a place where I could grow and help others grow, too.

These experiences were also critical in shaping my relationships. Interacting with other authors opened doors and created friendships that have enriched my life in immeasurable ways. And in the process of self-care, I found that my passion for wellness was contagious, positively affecting those around me.

In hindsight, these turning points didn't just set me on a new path; they equipped me with the tools I needed to navigate it successfully. They taught me the value of community, the importance of self-love, and most critically, the immeasurable impact of living a life rooted in purpose.

This journey hasn't been without self-doubt and setbacks. I can't count the number of times I found solace in prayer when the weight of uncertainty felt unbearable. Scriptures became my sanctuary, reminding me that even when we're lost, we're never truly alone. It is my faith that nudged me to reflect, not just on what I want to achieve, but on the kind of person I aspire to be, the values I want to uphold, and the impact I wish to have.

Finding purpose isn't an abstract quest solved only by self-help gurus. It's a practical journey that you can embark upon, one step at a time. I'm here to share the real, actionable steps that helped me align with my true calling. Think of these as your own personalized toolkit for purpose-discovery.

Invest In Yourself. It's like planting seeds for a future you can't even fully imagine yet. When you put your time, money, and energy into something meaningful, you're essentially saying, "I am worth it." For me, joining that multi-author book was a game-changer. It was more than just a financial commitment; it was an act of self-love and a statement of self-belief. Beyond the dollars and cents, the return on investment included invaluable networking opportunities, personal growth, and a newfound sense of confidence.

Courses, books, or experiences that resonate with you aren't just purchases; they're investments in your own 'personal stock.' Each time you invest, you add layers to your identity, enriching your skillset and widening your perspective. This, in turn, enables you to offer more to the world, whether it's through your writing, your relationships, or just the enriched way you approach life. So go ahead and bet on yourself— you're the safest gamble you'll ever make.

Embrace the Power of Community. When I decided to connect with other authors in the collaboration book I was part of, it wasn't just a casual move; it was a strategic step toward building a network of like-minded individuals. Those connections became far more than just professional contacts—they evolved into friendships, a reliable sounding board, and coaches and mentors in some cases. This community has been indispensable in amplifying my purpose; their collective wisdom and diverse experiences enriched my own journey.

We often overlook the importance of emotional support, but in a creative field like writing—or in life in general—it's golden. In times of self-doubt or when facing hurdles, it's this tribe that rallies around you, providing constructive criticism, encouragement, or even just a listening ear. The network effect of a strong community is exponential; it can open doors you didn't even know existed. So never underestimate the power of your tribe; it can be the catalyst that takes your career, and personal well-being, to new heights.

Listen to Your Inner Voice. For me, taking that time off from the daily grind to do some soul-searching was both liberating and transformative. Amid the chaos of responsibilities and deadlines, it's so easy to lose sight of what makes our hearts sing. Diving deep into my motivations, fears, and dreams was, honestly, a bit nerve-wracking, but it was also like flipping on a light switch in a dim room. Not only did this introspective pause help me discover my passion for coaching writers, but it also highlighted a critical gap in my life: the need for self-care. By putting those realizations into action, I was able to align my daily life and work with what truly mattered to me. And you know what? That kind of alignment is invaluable. It impacts not just your sense of satisfaction, but it elevates your performance in every facet of life—professional and personal. So, give your inner voice the microphone; what it has to say could change your life.

Faith and Service. For me, my faith has been like an anchor, providing a sense of stability and peace even when life gets stormy. It's not just about believing; it's about living those beliefs in actionable ways. My role as a faith leader has been incredibly rewarding, providing tangible proof that I'm making a positive impact, whether it's through mentoring, teaching, or community outreach.

So, if you're a person of faith, don't just keep it as an abstract concept. Actively engage with it. Make time for spiritual connection, be it through prayer, meditation, or other practices. This nurtures your soul and provides mental clarity. Take it a step further by getting involved in volunteer work or mentoring. Offering your skills and time to causes that resonate with you is not just fulfilling; it's a way to live out your faith in a meaningful manner. The beauty of faith coupled with service is that it creates a ripple effect, improving not just your life but also touching the lives of others in profound ways.

Being Strong Enough to Bend: Purpose isn't a destination; it's an evolving journey. In reality, purpose is more like a river, constantly flowing and changing its course as it adapts to the landscape. Thinking of it as an evolving journey takes the pressure off "having it all figured out" and gives you the freedom to adapt, grow, and pivot. When you see these steps as signposts rather than a rigid roadmap, you make room for serendipity, for unexpected turns that may just lead you to incredible vistas you never knew existed.

It's the flexible approach that allows you to engage fully with life, to be open to opportunities, and to learn from setbacks. This dynamic view ensures you're not just setting a course but enjoying the ride, embracing the highs and navigating the lows with resilience. Your journey toward purpose isn't a straight highway but a winding path with surprises around every bend—each adding its own unique touch to your ever-evolving story. So buckle up and embrace the adventure that is your purposeful life!

As I look back on my journey of self-discovery, it's almost like staring at a before-and-after picture—one where the external changes are subtle, but the internal transformation is groundbreaking. Finding my purpose has been a metamorphosis that's turned my ordinary days into a tapestry of joyful moments, taking actions that scared the hell out of me and impactful connections.

Before, my days were a checklist of tasks to be completed, each tick mark a tiny but empty victory. Now, each task feels saturated with intention and meaning. Whether I'm mentoring someone on their self-care journey or working with authors at Action Takers Publishing, the sense of purpose propels me forward. There's an undeniable thrill in seeing aspiring writers evolve into published authors, but the fulfillment runs deeper. It's in knowing that I've played a part in helping someone else achieve their dream, which in turn cements my own purpose and elevates my day-to-day living to something far more gratifying.

Promoting self-care and helping women become self-care rockstars themselves has also added a layer of richness to my life that I hadn't anticipated. In uplifting others, I uplift myself. The joy isn't just in the milestones but also in the small, everyday victories. Every interaction is a validation, a reassuring pat on the back from the universe that whispers, "Well done, my good and faithful servant."

Lastly, the synergy between my personal and career goals has created a harmonious balance I didn't think was possible. For me, this synergy has been like discovering the sweet spot where my passion, skills, and impact intersect. And the ripple effects are astounding. Professionally, relationships have shifted from transactional encounters to meaningful connections, laying the groundwork for not just business success but also personal growth. Fostering friendships with fellow authors and building a supportive community has not only enriched my career but also deepened my personal life.

Let's not underestimate the goldmine that is internal peace. It's as if finding my purpose has sent waves of positive energy into all facets of my life. That internal tranquility radiates outward, benefiting not just me but also my family. When I'm balanced and at peace, it creates a harmonious environment at home, enriching our collective well-being. So, this isn't just about ticking boxes on a career or life checklist; it's about crafting a lifestyle that's both fulfilling and sustainable, one that allows every aspect of your life to flourish.

To sum it up, finding my purpose hasn't just rearranged the pieces of my life; it's turned the landscape into a richer, more vibrant playing field. Every move feels deliberate, every decision easier to make, because they're guided by a newfound clarity. And in that clarity, I've discovered not just the joy of living, but the profound satisfaction of living a life that truly matters.

In this journey we call life, finding your purpose is like finding your compass—it doesn't tell you the destination, but it sure makes navigating a lot easier. Trust me when I say that uncovering your purpose is akin to unlocking a treasure chest of joy, fulfillment, and a sense of mission that elevates even the mundane aspects of daily living. For me, this meant transforming from someone who was constantly chasing tasks to becoming a woman deeply rooted in intention, one who finds profound joy in writing, publishing, and even simple hobbies like painting.

What I want you to take away from my journey is that finding your purpose is not a luxury; it's a necessity for a life well-lived. It is the lens through which you see the world, influencing your actions, relationships, and even your sense of self-worth. It's what transformed me into a self-care rockstar, allowing me to serve others more effectively while nurturing my own well-being. My days are now aligned with my aspirations, both personal and professional, resulting in a life that feels not just lived, but cherished.

If you're still on the quest for your purpose, take heart. Know that it's okay to feel lost sometimes; even the most scenic routes have their share of twists and turns. Keep investing in yourself, be it through education, relationships, or even soul-searching. Don't underestimate the power of community, and never shy away from opportunities that resonate with you—even if they scare you a little. Above all, keep the faith. Your purpose is out there, waiting to turn your life from a monochrome picture into a vivid masterpiece.

In the immortal words of Ralph Waldo Emerson,

"The purpose of life is not to be happy. It is to be useful, to be honorable, to be compassionate, to have it make some difference that you have lived and lived well."

So go out there and live well, by finding and embracing your true purpose.

Sally Larkin Green

Sally Green is the Vice President of Author Development at Action Takers Publishing. She works with writers to help them develop their stories and become bestselling authors.

At the age of 58, Sally realized that she was really good at taking care of everyone else, but really bad at taking care of herself. So, she embarked on a journey of self-care that began with investing in herself and contributing to a multi-author book. Sally is an inspirational speaker, a multiple times International Bestselling Author, and is in the process of writing her own book.

Connect with Sally at www.ActionTakersPublishing.com.

CHAPTER 3

From Health Struggles to Purpose: A Journey of Healing and Entrepreneurship

Christine Lennips

For my family...who's love, caring, and support in so many ways is truly appreciated.

The diagnosis: "Parasites are killing off your brain cells."

Imagine that you are 16 years old and experiencing low-grade headaches which would come and go four to five times throughout the day. You don't have a lot of energy for being a teenager. Your bones and muscles seem to ache far too often, and those headaches are becoming tiresome.

That is what was happening to me!

I tried to do as much work on the dairy farm as I could, before and after school. I often was in the house helping with those chores instead, because it seemed to be easier on my body than working with some of the barn and milking tasks. The lack of energy made it challenging to do even basic chores, as another low-grade headache could come on and "take me down" for one to three hours. And of course, I still had homework to do on many evenings. By the time the school year had ended, I had only passed two of my five classes. I had been a good student, so this was not typical! I would have loved to have been a fly on the wall as the teachers discussed this decline in my grades. The typical reasons for such declines did not align with what was happening to me. Looking at my report card, all these years later, there was all-around disappointment in my effort and end results.

So, I was off to the medical doctor to try to find the reason this was happening. He suggested an over-the-counter pain reliever for the headaches. No further tests were even suggested. There was limited success with that treatment, and of course, there was the frustration of not knowing what was causing these headaches.

Growing up on a dairy farm, parasites were something that you could catch quite easily either from the animals or the manure. They could be introduced to you by touching the animals or a tail swish across the face. We had a dog and several barn cats to play with. So, of course, you can get them from your pets, too. In addition, you can get parasites in your food or water. Parasites tend to absorb most of the nutritional benefits of the food and supplements one consumes, denying you the health benefits the body desperately needs. Being around the animals and working on the dairy farm would have contributed to my parasite issue. The parasites had moved from the bowel and traveled to my brain!

It was my chiropractor who recommended that I pursue the natural health avenue. He felt that I was not responding well to the normal chiropractic care protocol for a teenager, either. His thought was that the person that my parents were consulting for their health, may be able to figure out something to help me.

So, off I went for another opinion. It was the iridologist and herbal specialist who gave me that horrible prognosis. It was scary, but now I had an explanation! They recommended that I start taking some herbal and nutritional supplements to build and cleanse different parts of my body. The intention was to give my body the support that it needed to target these affected body systems.

As I became consistent with taking my supplements, my body began to start working better for me.

We were addressing the parasite issue, but there were other things that needed to happen in order to be successful. For example, I had to improve bowel function so that the parasites could leave my body once they were killed off. We had to do that gently to protect my gut from the poisonous toxins the parasites were putting off while dying. And no one wants the surprise attacks that can cause. My brain was affected too, and I needed additional help to improve my focus and memory. I wanted to go back to school and continue with my high school studies. My whole future was at stake here, my education along with my health. At that time, I had wanted to be a teacher. I had no clue if that was even possible anymore, considering my poor grades.

As my health was improving, people started noticing. My energy was increasing … I was becoming a teenager again. Not a typical rebellious one, but a teenager who could bounce around and do things, someone who was living and enjoying their young life. I was able to handle tasks on the farm with more ease. Of course, I was truly thankful for where I was at. Waiting just one year later, things could have been a lot harder to deal with.

I decided not to pursue continuing education in a college or university after high school. I repeated my grade 12, with additional courses and improved grades. Remember my chiropractor? I started working part-time after school in his office. He was now my boss, too! I even continued with grade 13. While in my last year of high school, I took classes in the morning and worked part-time for two to three afternoons per week in the chiropractic office.

When that schooling was complete, I began working in his other chiropractic office location, as well. I was now working part-time to full-time hours.

Being immersed in the office setting with patients wanting to maintain and improve their health, I was experiencing more interaction with people on a variety of levels. Of course, in his practice, health was very important. He would ask me questions about what herbs were best for certain health issues or symptoms. Or, what else does this herb do? Sometimes he would discuss a concern and ask for my suggestions. I would research, if needed, and let him know what I had found out that could help. Later, I realized that he knew the answers. He was just helping me to expand my knowledge, develop my ability to research and grow my thirst for learning.

When I was 21, I attended a training school with the product line company I had been using for five years. I expanded my knowledge about their herbal and nutritional supplements. I learned about the various properties of herbs and the body systems that they support.

I was being trained to use muscle testing, one of the methods that I had been experiencing while selecting my supplements. During this training, I developed more techniques for muscle testing (Applied

Kinesiology). This is a great way to determine which supplements are best for your body system that needs support. You can test using your arm or hand. When you ask the body a question, its own energy gives you the answers!

I started to study iridology (the analysis of the iris – the coloured part of the eye). They say that the eyes are the windows to the soul. It is possible for me to look into your eyes with a lighted magnifying glass and be able to see the weaknesses that are passed down to you from your parents and grandparents. The markings in the iris are related to different parts of your body. This is used to be able to learn what weaknesses are present or may become issues in the future, if not require attention now. Remember that this was one of the methods used to help me figure out what was happening with my health five years earlier.

At 21 years of age, this total immersion of information and pieces of training moved me into a whole new world. I was looking to start a part-time job to go along with working at the chiropractic office. It would be something I could do working from home. I officially joined the herbal company three months later. I was one of their youngest distributors in the company!

Little did I know that a health issue five years earlier that could have killed me if left unchecked, was leading me to helping others. Aside from my health improvements, improved self-esteem came alongside this process. This shy girl was growing and developing into a home business entrepreneur.

A few years later, I had the opportunity to train under Dr. Bernard Jenssen. He was a chiropractor and was one of the pioneers of iridology. This was the beginning of my learning from many other trainers on various topics and occasions. Continuing education was in my future. I was constantly being educated more about herbs, natural health, and different holistic modalities, for ways to help my clients. I was learning more about how the body works. Rather than taking a few years of schooling, I was learning while I was working with clients, and learning from them.

As I was learning more and sharing often with others about my own experiences, I was starting to build a clientele. People wanted to know how their health could be improved after they learned of the success that I had experienced using these products. I loved being able to help people, or, should I say, I LOVE helping people!

Something that I learned very quickly is that we are all unique. I had access to over 200 products within my favourite product line and most of my clients were not doing the same program. Each one had slightly different symptoms or, if they had similar symptoms, there was a different reason or root cause that needed to be addressed in order to address those health symptoms. This soon became a driving force in my business. The uniqueness of each client meant that there was no cookie-cutter program. Every person needed their own personal attention and was working with products specifically geared for their needs, at the present time. This allowed me to address the needs of the big strong person, to the more petite body by simply having them adjust dosage and target their body's needs.

Yes, time has gone along in my business, 35 years so far! There are many things that I have been noticing. Stress levels are going up, and the desire for natural health options is also increasing. Although people value medical opinions, they still prefer to put natural products into their bodies rather than pharmaceutical, chemically made-up prescriptions and over-the-counter medications.

I have found that getting at the root cause of a health symptom is the best way to help someone. Rather than doing a cover-up job, or chasing symptoms, I go after what the root cause is for a client's particular issue or concern. For example: if the client wants to lose weight, I need to look at metabolism, glandular system, digestion, and how the bowels are working, and may need to do liver detoxification or help cleanse the urinary system. This is alongside the food they consume. There are weight loss products that my line carries, but that might not be where we start. Another example is low energy. There are five different body systems involved—digestive, circulatory, immune, glandular, and hepatic (liver, gallbladder, blood). We need to figure out which systems need support so that you can increase your energy, rather than just throwing energy drinks, coffee, etcetera, at your concern. You want to have energy so that you can LIVE your life ... DO the activities you want with ease. You want a great quality of life!

Another thing that I find interesting with my clients is that a lot of them benefit from doing a liver detox twice a year. The body chooses the best time to do tasks. So, in my business, I could say that I have a seasonal business. I get extremely busy for the first two weeks of each new season. This is when my clients all want to come into my office and adjust their programs to what the body works with for the next season. A lot of my client's bodies want liver/gallbladder detoxification in Spring and Autumn, while in Summer and Winter, their bodies prefer glandular work, along with structural and nervous system support. With everyone being unique and each person having slightly different issues, every day seems to be a bit different in my office. There is no opportunity for boredom.

When the recent pandemic occurred, my business had to change. Within the first year, on three different occasions, I had to close my office doors to my clients. There was no way I was going to be able to continue doing my business if this was what was going to continue. I did not have a way to help them while they were outside, and I was inside; other than selling them products, that they could order directly from the company or offering carport pick up from outside of my office. But the muscle testing (where I was physically touching their hand) couldn't be done if they weren't able to be in my office. This is when I learned that it was possible to do applied kinesiology from a distance or virtually. With that option, I could work with my clients who could not come into my office. This new opportunity was going to allow me to expand my business outside of a two-hour drive radius. I then chose to expand my potential client base to include all of Canada and the United States. Since I have room for more new clients. I am expanding my business to full-time! Going forward, I will be offering group and one-on-one attention.

My ill health started me on my journey. My improved health made me want to help others who weren't getting the help they wanted and needed.

God wove a silver thread into my DNA to make sure that I looked after my own health and began a search into learning how to help myself improve. There was a path I was destined to follow. This led me to help others along the way. A business career began because a teenager refused to quit on herself or others. Is every day rosy? No. But I love helping others improve on their health, just like I got to improve on mine. If I do not open my mouth and share with others, I am doing them a disservice. Someone helped me and I am meant to help others with their health journey.

Who knew that a health issue back when I was a teenager would set in motion my ability to find my purpose … and follow it through? I may be 57 years old now, but I plan on working for at least another 20 years. There are so many more people looking for help, and I am here to help them!

Christine Lennips

Christine Lennips is a well-being expert and herbalist who has been practicing for over 35 years. She is dedicated to helping people achieve optimal health and wellness. With a passion for natural remedies and supplements, she began her journey as a practitioner after experiencing incredible results with her own health.

As she continued to expand her knowledge and skills, she developed a deep understanding of the body's interconnected systems and the underlying root causes of various health symptoms. Her unique approach combines a range of modalities, alongside herbal medicine, to address the whole person and create a personalized plan for each individual.

She lives in Hanover, Ontario Canada with her husband Robert. They both enjoy nature, and she loves her herbal business.

Christine's approach and extensive experience have helped countless individuals overcome a wide range of health concerns. Her commitment to ongoing education and her dedication to her clients' well-being has made her a trusted and valued member of the holistic health community.

Whether you're struggling with a chronic health condition or simply looking to optimize your overall wellness, she can help you achieve your goals and live your best life!

Connect with Christine at https://www.knocard.app/itsaboutyou.

CHAPTER 4

How I Listened to My Soul, and Found Everything I Ever Wanted

Dr. Christy Matusiak

I dedicate this chapter to anyone struggling to push past the fear of failure. To anyone working day after day, unfulfilled to make ends meet. Find your spark and find your joy. You CAN make your dreams come true.

For as long as I can remember, I was interested in holistic health, and this was long before it was trendy. I was fascinated by the nature vs. nurture concept. How much of who we are (our health/constitution) is based on our genetics? And how much is attributed to our chosen lifestyles and upbringing?

My college admissions essay depicts clearly who I was, and what I wanted, all long even before I consciously found my purpose:

In the field I am interested in, there are many options. I plan to double major in kinesiology (exercise science) and psychology. This gives me flexibility in a career choice. At this point, I'm aspiring to be a personal trainer. I want the background in psychology, so I can help an individual's mental health, as well as physical health for a holistic approach. I feel that this line of work would suit me well considering my dedication to serving and caring for others in need ...

When in college, I was the kid that when I would feel sick, I would intuitively not eat certain things, and high dose myself on vitamin C for a few days. Magically, my illnesses would only last two to three days. This was common sense to me, although my roommate made fun of me incessantly for it. Little did I know, this intuition of mine was an entire field of health and medicine that was my true calling.

I graduated from my undergraduate program earning a Bachelor of Arts degree in biology and psychology. I changed my primary major from exercise science to biology, as it offered a deeper dive into the sciences and more options overall. Plus, I felt the education in that department was better. Yet again, when I graduated, most people thought I was crazy putting those two fields of study together. I would frequently get: "BIOLOGY AND PSYCHOLOGY! What do they have to do with each other?" Today, mind-body medicine is clearly important and connected. The term holistic is commonplace. Back then, people thought I had lost my mind. But I was grateful that my first job out of school was a great one. I worked for Abbott Laboratories in the Diagnostics Division as a quality technician. I ensured labels were on products, bottles weren't leaking, and manufacturing systems were in compliance. It was boring. And, it certainly didn't fulfill me on a deep level, making a difference in the world. But it was steady, reliable, and a decent income for a 22-year-old.

After a little over a year in that entry-level position, I began interviewing for other positions within the company. The one I remember most clearly was a lab position in the Pharmaceutical Division. They asked me in the interview, "Where do you see yourself in five years?"

I replied, "Honestly, in five years, I would love it if I were in a more clinical supportive setting, where I could help people focus on their health and the prevention of disease—to the point that people may not NEED medications, because they aren't sick."

My answer was my honest truth. It was, and always had been, my passion. It lit me up to talk about it. And yet, remember where I was interviewed! The *pharmaceutical* division of a *pharmaceutical* company! I don't think they cared for my perspective. But not getting that job was exactly what I needed.

Shortly after that time, I met a chiropractor who had done a health talk: Dr. Justin Tossing. My mom had seen his presentation and recommended I check him out as his content seemed, "right up my alley." Upon meeting him and learning about chiropractic and holistic medicine, I found EXACTLY what I was looking for my entire life, but didn't know it existed. I began working for him part-time, a few days per week after my job at Abbott. I learned so much and enhanced my own health in the process of working for him. Through some testing and energy work, he suggested I take wheat gluten and dairy out of my diet. Now, let me explain—bread and cheese were my all-time FAVORITE foods. I was getting married in a few months, and besides wanting to lose weight, I had eczema patches on my arms that were somewhat substantial. He felt the dietary change would help. I agreed to play along for two weeks and see what happened.

I must say, I felt pretty amazing during those two weeks! My skin was clearer, my energy was better, and I just felt overall healthier, happier, and full of vitality! But, I still wasn't convinced. After all, I had also increased my water intake during that time, began exercising more, and it was summer during which time I felt better, anyway. So, after my two weeks were up, I said: "Screw it. I'm gonna eat whatever I want. I don't buy it." That afternoon, I attended a family party, so I feasted on a giant plate of mostaccioli—filled with gobs and gobs of mozzarella cheese, and decadent pasta. It was heavenly. But literally, within an hour, my body started itching. Not the kind of itching where hives are present and you have a clear anaphylactic reaction to something. It was the buzzing, subtle itchiness associated with my eczema. The internal torment where you do your best to resist the intractable itch. The kind where there is no rash until you scratch it. After all, eczema is *the itch that rashes*, not *the rash that itches*. It was then that I made the correlation between what I had avoided for two weeks, and just eaten loads of. I thought, "Ok, maybe there is something to this." From that moment, I did the best I could to avoid those foods for close to a year. Was I perfect? No, but I probably was 90 percent or better for the whole year. And the result? No more eczema. Seriously—gone. That was back in 2005–2006. And I haven't had an issue with an eczema outbreak in well over a decade. I don't eat a ton of those things anymore, in general, but I'm not neurotic about avoiding them either.

While I was working part-time with Dr. Tossing, he taught me everything I ever wanted to know about the holistic health world. Like I said, it felt like I was called home. This wellness field was a part of my soul. He taught me about muscle testing, food sensitivities, nutrition, the nervous system, and more. I was convinced I knew what my next steps were. So, I started looking into nutrition school programs. He advised me against that, but nutrition school was much cheaper than a chiropractic degree! Then something happened ...

Fate stepped in.

Abbott had a huge layoff in July 2005. I remember the day we all knew it was happening. One by one, I watched as my bosses and other co-workers were called to walk the long hallway where at the end they were met by two suited Human Resource professionals with their folders, severance package, and invitation to leave the company. It was an intense, anxiety-filled day. When my turn arrived, I was emotional. I had a knot in my stomach the whole time. That hallway walk seemed to take years. But at the end of it, while I was filled with emotion, fear, and uncertainty, the end of that hallway simultaneously represented something else: Freedom. No more signatures on boring manufacturing lines. No more headaches over a label being crooked. This was my green light to pursue my dreams. I knew more than ever before what this quote meant:

When one door closes, another opens.
~Alexander Graham Bell

And it was the door to my future that had opened.

I began chiropractic school in May 2006. Dr. Tossing was my mentor through most of my time in school. Yet, I remember his eternal words, as I was getting ready to enter the chiropractic program at National University of Health Sciences (NUHS). I was filled with excitement to learn even more about all he had taught me over the last year. And he says, "By the way, you don't learn this in school."

39

WHAT!??

What do you mean by, "You don't learn this in school?" He was referring to the work of Applied Kinesiology (AK). This is a system of diagnosis that connects muscles to organ systems, meridians, and emotions. The system was created by Dr. George Goodheart and has grown substantially since 1964. Yet it was *this* work that sparked that soul calling within me. So, how is it possible that something so powerful and life-changing in the world of health isn't taught in school?

The truth is that it was taught—just not as part of the regular chiropractic curriculum. AK courses were offered as part of the postgraduate weekend seminars, and of course, were at an extra cost. Still, I jumped right in. By my second trimester at school, I became the AK Club president and worked to run all the extra seminars. I sought out doctors to come and teach 100-hour courses, and more. Was it stressful? ABSOLUTELY. But nothing in my life had ever seemed so worth it. The countless hours of studying for exams, taking boards, and doing clinical rotations were often draining and brutal. And amazing. I'm forever grateful to my husband who supported me through all of it!

I graduated chiropractic school from NUHS in August 2009. I was filled with a burning passion to serve and heal the world. I got my practice together and opened my doors in October. Then, a few short weeks later, life took an unexpected turn.

I was pregnant.

Now, this was fantastic news. Just one to two years before, I had struggled getting off birth control, experienced irregular periods, and received a diagnosis of Polycystic Ovarian Syndrome (PCOS). Some practitioners would have said I wouldn't be able to get pregnant at the time. Luckily, having the holistic background and knowledge I did, I was able to forgo the western medicine recommendations and bring my

40

cycles back into regularity without the assistance of any medications! I'm thankful that I can now support my female patients through similar struggles!

At that time, while I was excited to start a family, and grateful that my body had normalized and was functioning well, I had no idea what to do. My focus shifted from starting a practice to starting a family. How on Earth could I do both? (I could write an entire other chapter on that, alone!) Long story short—I didn't do both. For a long time. I held deep subconscious beliefs that I couldn't be a successful doctor/healer/ business owner, and be a good/present mom at the same time. Clearly, that isn't true. But that is what belief systems are, right? The acronym is **BS** for a reason. Emotions, by definition, aren't rational. I spent 2010-2018 working <u>very</u> part-time. Like five–ten hours per week, at best. In those years, I had three sons—in 2010, 2013, and 2016. And each time that I would start to think, the baby was getting older, and I could again focus on myself and my career, I'd become pregnant again.

While those years came with many financial, mental, emotional, and physical struggles, I truly believe that every experience carries with it a lesson. It's through those challenges that I developed the utmost respect and reverence for moms crushing it every day. Working? Stay-at-home? It doesn't matter. It's the hardest job in the world and comes with no pay, no respect, and no recognition. I'm out to change that. Within my life circumstances, I learned empathy and understanding on how else to support people, especially women, through various health and life challenges. Moms often put their own needs last as a self-sacrifice. You wouldn't believe how many moms bring in their children for treatment, and during the course of the kid's appointment, they say, "When he/she is done, I should probably make an appointment for me." Why do women constantly make themselves and their own needs an afterthought? It is through these last several years that my truest calling evolved: Supporting moms and their growing families with holistic healing work.

This is not to say I don't treat men. Or women without children and families. I LOVE what I do. It's clearly a passion of mine to meet people where they are, hear their story, and through the right balance of emotional, energetic, chiropractic, nutritional, and lifestyle work, watch miracles happen. But, as I have grown and evolved in my journey, as a mother and doctor, I feel at my core the connection to help moms reach their greatest potential in this life. Physically. Emotionally. Nutritionally. Spiritually. In any way that matters to them. Because if moms, the leaders, and managers of the home aren't healthy and thriving, the entirety of the family will suffer.

I authored *Coordinating the Chaos – Through Birth and Burnout*, published in July 2021. This was intended to support the newly postpartum woman through the early struggles and demands on motherhood, while also offering guidance and holistic tips for the baby in the first one to two years of his/her life. Anyone with children knows that the chaos doesn't stop after the child exits the infancy stage. So, book two—*Coordinating the Chaos—Through Toddlerhood, Toilets, and Tantrums* is scheduled to be published by early 2024! And my plan is to continue the series as long as needed to offer that village of support to mamas at any stage

Holistic health is so popular now that almost everywhere, you can find a practitioner practicing functional medicine. Or a therapist touting the importance of trauma work. Or a chiropractor that addresses your whole system. But, those of us that truly connect with you, treat the SPIRIT of the individual. We hear your life story, history, trauma and more. Connecting to determine the best course of action to aid in the healing at the deepest level possible. Doing that with moms, who then pass that healing down energetically to their families. There is literally no greater joy for me. I watch miracles and transformations in the lives of my patients every day. To think, without that fateful Abbott layoff, I may have missed out. I am eternally grateful for my journey of life.

I encourage anyone reading this to think about the passions you used to have. What were you excited about as a kid? Before you got scared and chose a paycheck over your dreams? I get it. I've been there. I almost threw in the towel on my chiropractic practice when my third son was three years old and I still hadn't worked through my mental challenges about running a business and being a good mom. But I got through it. With hard work, dedication, and lots of NET (neuro-emotional technique). If you have any stressors or patterns that have shown up in your life, time and time again, this system is so powerful to help your energy and nervous system clear the past patterns and traumas so you can respond instead of react. The more power you have over your life, the more you can execute on your dreams. And find your purpose. I'm grateful I have found mine. And I'm here to help you find yours!

Dr. Christy Matusiak

Dr. Christy Matusiak is a holistically-driven chiropractic physician practicing in Wilmette, IL, with Integrated Holistic Healthcare. She has spent the last decade helping patients overcome autoimmune conditions, digestive issues, hormonal imbalances, musculoskeletal pain, chronic inflammation, and more. She focuses on identifying the root cause of these conditions by addressing all areas of health (physical, nutritional, emotional, and energetic).

She hosts the YouTube channel, Dr. Christy Cares where she shares videos with secrets on living a naturally healthy life. She also authored the book "Coordinating the Chaos – Through Birth and Burnout," supporting the newly postpartum mother through life, and helping her create the mental clarity to be present for her growing family. Dr. Christy shares her own experiences and those of patients, to guide women through this stage of life with ease! The book also provides holistic tips on maintaining your baby's health! She's currently working on part two of the series with tips on coordinating the chaos through toddlerhood! Expected to be published in 2024!

Dr. Christy has been married for over 18 years and is a mom to three boys, ages 13, 10, and 7. She remains active with them and is committed to her own health and physical fitness. She recognizes that one's journey towards wellness is always evolving. Through this, she strongly values growth and self-reflection, believing that "health begins within each of us!"

Connect with Dr. Christy at https://linktr.ee/christymatusiakdc.

CHAPTER 5

Discovering Purpose Through the Process

Christy McCord

---

*I dedicate this to my wonderful kids, Skylar and Chayce,
my handsome husband, Jerry, and to my parents, Buddy
and Dianne. I also dedicate this to all of the mentors
the Lord has seen fit to place in my life throughout the
years. I could never list them all here, but I trust the Lord
remembers and I pray He touches their life in a special
way for their faithfulness to impart wisdom into my life.*

Significance and purpose go hand in hand. I'm convinced that everyone, in some form or fashion, is seeking significance in life. The very fact you are reading this book is evidence of that. We are all on a quest, whether consciously or subconsciously, for that *one thing* that assures us that we have value and purpose. And wouldn't it be nice if *our purpose* just magically dropped out of the sky and landed in our lap? Ah, but unfortunately, there's no fairy godmother to wave a magical wand, giving us a *bibbity bobbity boo*, and all of a sudden we are hit with the knowledge and understanding of the thing we call *our purpose*. As appealing as that may sound, we all know that is not how it works. I can hear the words of one of my favorite TV commercials now, "That is not how this works! That is not how any of this works!" Rather, I submit to you that true significance and purpose are found when we submit our will to a will that is much higher than our own, and we commit to the process.

Don't get me wrong. As a born-again believer in Jesus Christ, I do believe that I am called by God for *His purposes* and that every person is created in the image and likeness of God and is born with very distinct, God-given giftings and callings. *However*, it's only when I began putting action to my faith on the daily, in this real world that I live in, that I began to discover and develop the giftings and callings that work together to fulfill the purpose(s) of God in my life. Learning how to appropriate my unique giftings and callings to overcome the challenges of everyday life, offering solutions to problems, rising above the fray, and pressing on toward the purpose for my life is what makes life an adventure worth living.

My search for significance and purpose began at a very early age in life. As a Christian, I have always believed I was created in the image and likeness of my Creator. However, it's been a bit of a journey to get to that place of *finding purpose*. Purpose wasn't something I just inherently knew, but rather something I discovered in the process.

As a young kid, I had a profound understanding that life on this earth is but *a vapor*. I knew I was gifted by God, and I sought to find significance in just about everything I put my hands to because I wanted to be sure I was fulfilling my *God-given purpose* before my time was up. I wanted to please God with my life! As I am sure many people can relate, I was in Junior High when I really began struggling with and questioning my purpose. I was teased mercilessly for being an *overachiever*. And, while I had the drive to discover my purpose and walk in it, whatever *it* was, the struggle was very real. I was awkward and perceived as too serious, too different, and too square compared to my peers. I honestly hated Junior High so much that I can still recall sitting in my bedroom and thinking, "If I just sit still here on this bed, in a blink of an eye I'll be grown, and *this* will be over and done forever." I performed that exercise more times than I care to admit during my young life.

In those moments, as an immature kid, I chose to embrace the mindset of a victim rather than hold fast to the Lord's promise that He would make a way for me when there seemed to be no way. Because of my immaturity, I had great difficulty seeing past my own self-pity and had no ability to wrap my brain around significance and purpose. I literally wished the years (the process) away when I found myself feeling invalidated, insignificant, or dealing with a difficult situation that I believed served no purpose and certainly wasn't validating. I really began to believe, "What's the point?" I had been told by every grown-up in my world that, "Time flies" and, "This too shall pass," and I was READY! Ready for this to pass. To somehow magically skip past the now and on to the next, whatever that was to be for me. I desperately wanted out of the process to get to the next.

Obviously, time did not magically disappear. In fact, the next day still came. And the next day after that. With the passing of time, I began to mature and understand that maybe, just maybe, my life's purpose is birthed through the process. Eventually, I came to the realization that I could not fulfill my purpose without going through a process and that my first course of action was to just start walking out the steps in faith before I had much understanding of the purpose.

Purpose, for me, is not some ethereal, magical place you must strive your entire life to find or achieve, and then suddenly life has meaning. Rather, I have come to an understanding that purpose is discovered in the daily grind of life. For me, it is cultivated as I live out my life day by day. One step at a time. Line upon line. Precept upon precept. Every day is an opportunity to build upon the circumstances, discoveries, challenges, and victories of the previous day. For years, I have preached to my children that there is a purpose in the process, but we must participate in the process.

I am fortunate to have parents who instilled in me the importance of a strong moral compass and brought me up through their own core values rooted in our Christian faith. Part of the walking out process for me has been understanding and cultivating my strengths, honestly acknowledging my weaknesses, and defining my own personal core values. Core values determine how I/we do the daily grind. They drive our passions and the vision we have for our lives, which leads to purpose.

As I've alluded to, from the days of my childhood, I always had a strong desire to seek, know and speak the truth. I'm extremely justice-oriented and have a passion to serve and come to the defense of the helpless and underserved. As flawed an individual as I am, I have always embraced a core value of integrity – doing what is right because it is right, keeping my word even to my own detriment at times and doing unto others as I would have them do unto me. I also learned that I have a gift of encouragement. I love to encourage and speak life over others. My mom has referred to me as the family pastor, at times, because I'm seldom at a loss for words, even in a time of mourning. Somewhat conversely, I can also be counted on to speak the truth in the face of a lie, or as I see it, which often doesn't turn out as well as I would like. Even the truth, spoken in love doesn't land well sometimes. I have also learned that speaking my perceived truth is hollow and pointless if it is not rooted and grounded in The Truth. But I digress.

Recognizing and stepping into my gifts opened the door for me to experience some of the most rewarding years of my life in servant ministry. For a season of seven years, on a weekly basis, I had the honor of leading a team of like-minded men and women in ministry for senior citizens confined to several nursing homes in my hometown. My giftings also led me to a highly fulfilling career in the legal sector, where I worked as a civil trial paralegal for nearly two decades.

My gifts and core values, cultivated while walking through the process, have opened the door to opportunities I could have never imagined. Including becoming the co-owner of a successful health and wellness supplement company whose core values are truth, integrity, and empowerment. Becoming an entrepreneur was only a dream when I was a kid, but it's a reality in which I now live.

Living daily from a place of abiding conviction and an overarching worldview with clear core values kept me grounded, and mostly sane, when being a mother of two amazing children was one of the highest purposes in my life. It is what motivates me to be the wife I'm called to be to my husband and to walk alongside of him, encourage him and together cultivate a marriage of love, honor, respect, and trust. Intentionally building a life on a foundation of true conviction opens the door to a life filled with purpose.

Life has a way of throwing curveballs into the equation along the way to purpose, so I am under no delusion that the process to purpose is all butterflies, ponies and popsicles. Along the way, as a young child, I suffered abuse at the hands of a man with evil intentions, suffered the loss of loved ones I just knew would live forever, divorced after 20 years of marriage, and have admittedly made some extremely poor choices and suffered the consequences for those choices. But the beauty of choosing to daily embrace The Truth and walk out each day with only the faith the size of a mustard seed is that there is REDEMPTION of my purpose. Redemption for me is two beautiful grown children with whom I have a great relationship, re-marriage to a man for whom I prayed very specifically, bonus kids and grandchildren, parents that remain steadfast and continue to speak truth and life over me and my family, new friendships and opportunities for ministry, a new career, and business ownership.

Even now, my mind will occasionally drift back to those specific moments, in my younger years, when I desperately wished life would just fast forward to the future. I am struck with the realization that the very thing I desperately wanted, indeed happened. Those days I so desperately tried to wish away have seemingly evaporated in the blink of an eye. In reality, of course, the days did not magically vanish. No. The days, months and years did not disappear. I lived and survived every second, every minute, every hour, every day, and every year that is now … poof! … gone! The awkward years of junior high and every other season in life that I knew as ugly or uncomfortable are now gone, but so are the many wonderful, glorious days full of adventure, growth, beauty, and excitement. Life truly is but a vapor.

You've heard it said:

Life is the culmination of the choices we make daily.

Sometimes we feel called or drawn to something, but we are unable to see the purpose in it. While I'm not saying that every unction or thought to pursue a thing is ordained or appointed for our life, it's often when we choose to begin walking out the process or path in front of us that we discover purpose.

Life is lived and purpose is defined in the process.

At the end of the day, to the best of my ability as a flawed human, I strive to live in accordance and obedience to

---

Seek His Kingdom first and His righteousness,
and all these things will be added unto me.
~Matthew 6:33

All these things in the context of scripture refer to all the things and anything that the Lord already knows we need. He not only knows that I need significance and purpose, but He has promised to provide it. I strive to walk confidently in the assurance that every day of the process is leading to His ultimate plan and purpose for my life.

Christy McCord

Christy McCord is a devoted mother, wife, and an inspiring advocate for health and wellness. With a heart for transformation and a deep-rooted commitment to holistic living, Christy has charted a remarkable journey from adversity to empowerment.

As a mother of two thriving grown children and a cherished wife to her biggest supporter, Jerry, Christy's family circle has expanded to include a blended family of six children and six grandchildren, with the promise of more to come.

Christy's transformative path began years ago when her own health quest led her to overcome remarkable challenges. Battling obesity and grappling with autoimmune disorders and various syndromes, Christy's determination drove her to seek answers beyond conventional medicine. Guided by a commitment to truth and the belief in the body's innate ability to heal, she found a holistic practitioner and mentor in Dr. Roby Mitchell, M.D. His teachings and protocols became foundational to her multi-year journey to regain her health.

Leaving a successful two-decade legal career as a civil trial paralegal, Christy's journey took a pivotal twist in 2015 when she partnered with Dr. Mitchell's enterprise, The PYR Less Group, known as Dr. Fitt, as COO. With the company's rebranding in 2022, Christy assumed the role of CEO and Co-owner of I'm Powered. She and her business partner are privileged to carry forward the legacy of Dr. Roby Mitchell.

Connect with Christy at www.impoweredhealth.com.

CHAPTER 6

No Regrets

Dara Bose

---

*This chapter is dedicated to my husband, my family, and
my best friend. To my husband, Bob, who has stood by
me through thick and thin as I have gone back to school,
changed careers, started businesses, and searched for my
purpose. It is your endless patience and support that have
helped make this possible.*

It was the first day of my dream job. I felt that I had finally made it!
After spending most of my adult life in a revolving door of jobs, I
had expected the doors to open, doves to come flying out, and a choir
of angels to sing. Of course, that didn't happen. The first couple of
months were amazing, but in less than a year's time, I began to feel the
darkness of my depression and anxiety creeping in. I had landed my
dream job. I had the big office, the fancy title, and the nice paycheck to

go with it. It was my dream job—the one thing I thought I needed to be happy and feel fulfilled.

Instead, I found myself dreading going to work. I was stressed, gaining weight, and—to be completely candid—drinking more than I care to admit. I was in a downward spiral and was losing myself along the way. It was affecting my family, too. I was lashing out at my husband and losing my patience with my kids. The path I was going down was dark, and I was struggling to keep from drowning.

Then, one evening as I was self-medicating with a bottle of wine and Facebook, I happened to scroll past a video, and it stopped me in my tracks. I had been praying for a life raft. I had been spending my life searching for that one thing that was going to make me happy—a new hobby, a direct sales company, my dream job. But I figured something out that night: there was no magic thing that was going to make me happy. I was solely responsible for my own happiness. It comes from inside of us. I just had to choose it. I could choose to be happy.

Choosing to be happy seems so easy, but how do we do it? I have heard all the inspirational quotes and seen all the memes about a positive mindset and positive thoughts. I tried the affirmations, but it was not enough. I figured if I wanted to be happy, I needed to do things that made me happy. I had to start by examining my life and the things that brought me joy. I always enjoyed learning, so I decided to start taking some classes and working on my own personal development. Classes, seminars, and books started to fill the time I had previously been using for mindlessly scrolling social media and drinking more wine than I should.

While on my journey of self-growth through personal development, I attended an online leadership event. At the time, I was working at a direct sales company and was rapidly growing a large team and making good money. During a breakout session, also focused on leadership, we discussed our *why*. Your *why* is the reason you do what you do. The reason you work so hard; the reason you continue when the times get tough or when you just don't feel like working. Most direct sales companies and multilevel marketing (MLM) businesses, including the one I was with, push new consultants to find their "why." So, when I found out we were going to spend an entire hour-long breakout session on this subject, I was a little disappointed since I had already figured out my *why*.

But I discovered something about myself that day. I never truly got deep enough into my *why* before that breakout session. I discovered my *why*, my *real why*. It comes from my fear of having regrets. Ever since losing my dad to suicide and harboring the feeling he may have regretted it, my *why* is to never have any regrets. I decided during that breakout session that I wanted to be a leader who takes big risks and leads my team without holding back.

When we returned to the main session from our breakouts, Dean Graziosi called me upfront. Did I mention this was an online event hosted by Dean Graziosi and Tony Robbins? Well, it was. So, Dean called me to be on camera in front of hundreds of people at this event to question me about my *why*. I wanted to hold back because I was partially awestruck being interviewed by one of my mentors, and afraid of speaking in front of hundreds of people. But I didn't want to have any regrets, so I went for it. He questioned me more about my *why* and being a leader, and I answered with something like this: "I believe I was chosen for this. God gave me these gifts, and one day when I meet my maker and he asks me, 'How did it go?' I can reply, 'I gave it my all. I used the gifts you gave me to my best efforts, and I have no regrets.' That is why I do what I do. I know I was given these gifts to make an impact on others in this world, to help them live their most abundant life."

This was a powerful revelation for me. It certainly helped keep me going when I wanted to quit from time to time, but it was still not enough. Something was still missing. I felt a heaviness, a darkness trying to creep back in. Even though I had found my *why,* I still wasn't happy. I was not being fulfilled. While I found a driving force to keep me going, I lacked happiness. I needed to step back and reexamine my life again.

I remember being told that to be happy, we need to be successful. Was I successful? Was that the missing piece? What was success? What does a successful person look like? Do they have a six-figure income job, or do they devote their life to charity work? Success looks different to everyone depending upon their beliefs and values. We spend so much of our lives trying to achieve someone else's version of success that we forget to even figure out what success means to us. That is what happened to me. I had all the things I was told I needed. I checked off all the boxes: a happy marriage, children, a nice house, and a nice car. We paid our bills and we went on vacations. I had to work hard, get a college degree, and get a good-paying job. That was the formula I thought I needed to achieve success, and that once I had those things, I would be successful. But I realized I was far from full—I was unfulfilled.

I was a great leader, and I did it well, but I felt like something was still missing. I now know that this feeling that something is missing sneaks in when your purpose or your calling is trying to get your attention. Your calling doesn't begin and end with your job. Just because you are really good at your job doesn't mean that it's your calling. And having a purpose or calling doesn't mean you have to quit your job, either. Your purpose or your calling is that thing that lights you up and brings you joy. It is the reason you get up in the morning. Your purpose or calling is in alignment with your values and your gifts. Your purpose could be as simple as being a friendly person. You could be that person who always holds the door open or smiles warmly at strangers. It can truly be that simple.

When we are busy hurrying through our day, checking off all those boxes for success—working, picking up and dropping off kids, paying the bills, all those things that society defines as success—we do it thinking we should be fulfilled when we're not. We feel like there must be something wrong with us, but there isn't. The problem is that we haven't taken the time out of our busy days to do what we are called to do. We are so preoccupied with our tasks that we fail to hold open that door. We failed to notice that the grocery store cashier looked like she had been crying. We didn't take the time to be that friendly smile those people may have needed, and now we feel like there is something missing. We missed our purpose, we didn't check that box, and we can feel it in our soul.

I was lacking my purpose.

I enjoyed being a leader, but most of all I enjoyed helping others. When I looked back at what I told Dean Graziosi during that leadership event, it became clear to me. I said, "I believe I was chosen for this. God gave me these gifts, and one day when I meet my maker and he asks me, 'How did it go?' I can reply, 'I gave it my all. I used the gifts you gave me to my best efforts, and I have no regrets.' That is why I do what I do. I know I was given these gifts to make an impact on others in this world, to help them live their most abundant life." It was right there! That was my purpose: to help others find abundance in their lives. While I was a leader with the company I was with, the one thing that brought me the most joy was helping other women discover their worth and helping them hit their own goals. It fueled me. Watching and helping other women rise, seeing their self-esteem and self-worth soar, made my soul sing!

Once I realized that my calling was to help others live their most abundant life, I started to put it into action. I looked for ways I could improve myself to help more people. I discovered that the biggest thing holding most women back was their mindset, including self-limiting beliefs and holding onto the past. Knowing this, I put in the work and became a certified NLP Practitioner and Life Coach.

I live out my purpose by coaching women using my NLP and Life Coach skills. I help them shed their old stories, break free of a negative mindset, and discover who they truly are. I also help women discover the power of their thoughts and emotions, by helping them understand how their thought process works. I have taken all my knowledge and experience and compiled it into a proven system to help others find their passion and purpose so they can stop merely surviving and start thriving. I figured it out, created a shortcut, and now I want to share what I know with others. I offer online and in-person workshops, and I even wrote a book on it.

Some people know what their purpose is right away, and others have a harder time finding it. People may have multiple purposes throughout their lives. I have a client who told me that her purpose in life was to be a mother and to raise her children, which is an amazing calling. However, now that her kids are all grown and out of the house, she feels empty and worthless. She certainly isn't worthless, but her feelings are valid. She was assigning her own self-worth and success to raising her kids, and now that they are adults, she doesn't have that driving daily purpose. I see this all the time in women, and once they start to feel this way, they seem to lose that spark that makes them truly alive. Just because her children are adults doesn't mean that she no longer has a purpose; it means it is time to find her next one.

I too haven't had the same purpose my entire life. Earlier, I was talking about that *dream job*. Well, for me, that dream job slowly turned into a nightmare job. Although I realized that I was responsible for my own happiness, I also continued to pray for a way out. I worked on my mindset and started my personal development journey, but I needed to find a new job. We had three young children who needed before- and after-school care since my mother-in-law could no longer provide this care due to illness. It just so happened that while on vacation with my husband in Tennessee, my best friend reached out to let me know that her church was looking for a part-time accountant. Since my degree was in accounting, I applied. This position would allow me to be home in the mornings to get the kids off to school and home in the afternoon when they got off the bus. The pay was exactly what we needed in addition to the extra money I made with the direct sales company to cover my salary. With this transition, I felt a shift in my calling.

I have been working at the church for years now. My position went from part-time to full-time, and my responsibilities have increased as well. I no longer work for that direct sales company, but I continue in a leadership role by leading a small women's group. In addition to my NLP and Life Coaching skills, I continue to grow in my faith. This brings me back to the shift in my calling. My husband and I were enjoying a beautiful evening by a fire on the top of a mountain back in Tennessee, and while we were sitting there talking about life and all things, I kept feeling a tug at my heart. He was asking me how he could be supportive of me in my coaching business and finishing my first book, and suddenly I just blurted out, "I want to be a Pastor!" He was not surprised and supported my calling, even though it had shifted. It was a surprise to me, though. I wasn't sure it was what I really wanted. I know that I am certainly not an expert and am still growing in my own faith, but after talking with my own Pastors and lots of contemplating, I decided to go back to school to get my degree in Psychology and become a Pastoral Counselor.

The core of my purpose is still the same—to help others live their most abundant life—but it just now includes faith. Sometimes our purpose can take us in directions we do not expect, but it's okay to make a shift. We are allowed to grow and change and with that, our purpose can change to align with who we are becoming. Keep in mind your own gifts when trying to find your purpose. God often gives us unique gifts to help us fulfill our purpose. Your gift may be simple. Your gift could be like mine, and you have an enormous capacity for caring for others. Maybe your gift is that you are an exceptional listener or friend. No matter what your gift is, it was given to you for a reason. You need to embrace it. If you are struggling to find your gift, ask your friends. They will tell you what it is.

Once you find your calling and embrace it, you can live life on purpose, with no regrets.

Dara Bose

Dara Bose is a certified NLP Practitioner, Life Coach, #1 International Best-Selling Author, and public speaker. She has spent years working on personal development while reaching top rankings in the multilevel marketing (MLM) industry. Through her work in MLM, she discovered her passion for building up other women and her purpose to help them thrive. The wife of a firefighter/paramedic and mother of three, Dara never ceases to amaze with finding time to support and uplift women in her community.

Whether through participating in small groups at church, organizing fundraising events, and everything in between, Dara represents her best self in all she does. She motivates women to seek their own selves through self-reflection, motivation, and friendship. Women seek out Dara for guidance regularly when working through difficult times, or just needing the support of another woman, mother, wife, or business owner. Constantly seeking to better herself and provide the best support she can to others, you can always find her reading a book or attending seminars that build her up and better equip her to share her messaging.

Dara is best known for the saying she uses regularly with her children and friends, which can be applied to anyone in most situations: "But did you die?" Most importantly, Dara wants all women to know, "You are worthy, you are beautiful, and you are meant for more."

You can connect with Dara at www.darabose.com.

CHAPTER 7

Poornatva –
From Fragmentation to Wholeness

Deepa Mahesh

I want to dedicate this chapter to the guiding light and the universe for nudging me to be in search of my purpose always. To my parents, teachers, and spiritual gurus who have given me lessons through pain and pleasure and led me on the path of inquiry and light. And gratitude to my inner light, which shines always, irrespective of the outer.

"I am born for big things and I want to make a big difference to humankind." Since I was 32 years old, this was what I always heard as a voice from within. With two children, a successful HR career and a supportive family, I had all that I could ask for. Growth in the corporate ladder seemed natural, but not effortless. Hence at 37, I began asking myself, "What is the purpose of my life? Is it only to work and parent? Is there more to it?" Reflection and contemplation were my second nature and this inquiry deepened as I began feeling unfulfilled in my career pursuits.

One fine day, I said, "There is more to it than this job, the money that pays my bills and the visiting card that boosts my ego." And I let go of a lucrative job for my *Search for Meaning and Purpose.*

The days that followed my exit from the corporate world were filled with a void and a sense of meaninglessness. Nothing to look forward to, nowhere to dress up and go to, nothing that springs me up from bed. Quite monotonous.

With every passing day, my desire to search for my purpose strengthened and it brought me to participate in a yearlong journey, "Foundation Course in Expressive Arts Therapy." It was a year full of self-exploration, healing, meeting my shadows, encountering my inner light and being in the company of a safe sisterhood.

In one of the art therapy sessions during the course, I was drawing a Tree Like Me and that led me to clearly meet and sense my Life purpose. My life purpose said, "Born to make a difference to humankind" and the visual I drew was a tree with strong roots, a thick trunk, numerous branches, and leaves with luscious red apples. The apples represented all the human beings I had transformed and there were many apples on the ground which were humans who had already transformed through my presence and were ready to walk on the path of their purpose.

Thus started my journey to live my life purpose.

Then began my search for the niche that I would be joyous serving. I explored working with high school students on their confidence, with college students on self-expression, with entrepreneur groups on body awareness, social institutions, old age homes, curative centres and more. I also set up an expressive arts therapy center where I took up client cases dealing with anxiety, depression, career dilemmas, relationship issues, emotional imbalances, and confidence issues, to name a few. I observed that clients who gravitated to me were corporate professionals in middle management, stuck in different areas of life and seeking a state of balance. This also opened doors for me to facilitate workshops in organisations based on arts and movement. A decade ago, these modalities were new and unheard of and there was a willingness to experiment. My mantra was, "Just keep exploring and doing." No opportunity was turned down by me. If I could understand the brief, I would strive to make a plan and reach the desired outcome. I experienced a lot of joy in experimenting with creative ways of delivering transformation to human beings. In that process, I honed my skills and discovered what my unique strengths were and how I could add value to professionals.

One practice I installed for myself, is a Daily Review. Before I retired each day, I would ask myself and journal "Did I live my life purpose?" Depending on the answer, I would plan my next action. I never stopped, to some, it may sound and look obsessive. I believe when the purpose feels aligned inside-out, passion turns into healthy obsession and it benefits self and others.

Leaving a routine path of corporate life and treading on the uncharted path of living my purpose was scary and confusing, too. Coupled with that was my personal style of decision-making and sensing the world, primarily with emotions and intuition. This always made it difficult for me to explain to others the rationale of my decisions. However, my family always had my back. They believed in my talents and knew I was chasing a dream that I was convinced about. They have always been a blessing in my growth path.

This journey had several roadblocks, more internal than external.

One of the biggest roadblocks was my *Inner Demons*. Demons in the form of limiting beliefs and thoughts. Growing up, I had nurtured a limiting belief that *I was not good enough and I had to strive hard to achieve anything big.* This was characterised by comparison with others in my field, irrespective of their age/experience/position. And the moment comparison would show me in a dim light, it would pull my emotions and energy down and I would crawl into self-doubt and self-loathing. I would also project power and competence onto others and put myself down, others would always look better than me and I was always short of being *good enough.* The root of this was uncovered in my journey with my Jungian analyst, I was as transparent as I could be with her, in fact, I learnt authenticity in that journey of personal therapy. And thereafter with shadow work with multiple professionals, I realised that my Power and Ambition, which were hiding in my shadows, had to be awakened and embraced. The journey of inner integration and stepping away from my inner fragmentation was a huge part of my self-exploration and so closely connected to my purpose. I had to be the cause of other's transformation, just like the journey I went through with myself. This was the preparation for executing my purpose effortlessly.

Another demon was the *lack of emotional balance.* Emotional trauma was a big part of my life from seven to twenty-five years of age. And that had caused a lot of damage to my sense of self, my confidence, and my inner stability. In my Self-Awareness journey, I chose to meet my emotions authentically, probably for the first time. Throwing emotional tantrums was my inner child's response to situations, I had to reparent my inner child, listen to her, and go through the process of adulting while offering self-love. I learnt the emotional balance process of emotional awareness, emotional expression, transforming disempowering emotions, and living emotionally trigger-free. This helped me recognise and set boundaries, which in turn helped me live my purpose with conviction and focus. I was in charge of my emotions. I built the muscle to transcend fear by tuning into the energy that comes from my purpose. I learnt to step out of sadness and rage by learning new ways to deal with anger. I also enrolled in a three-year certification course to study my biography and use the learnings to shift from blaming life to learning from my life, which I offer to my clients today. Living trigger-free was the big preparation for executing my purpose effortlessly.

Another big inner demon was *confusion*. Yes, I had discovered my purpose, but it didn't mean that I believed in it. What I saw as my purpose was just a visual, I had to be convinced and had to act in congruence with myself and others. My mindset was that of self-doubt, it didn't allow me to step into my purpose with conviction. One of the books that has made a profound impact on me since 2009, is Peter Senge's, *Fifth Discipline*. The discipline of Personal Mastery taught me that clarifying my vision and purpose is a continuous job and not a one-time affair. The moment I sensed confusion, I would go to the drawing board, draw my vision, and articulate my purpose. Ultimately the same energy would come up in different words. This enabled me to reinforce myself constantly. This also helped me reduce the external validation and trust in my internal intuition even more. I created a tombstone image and inscribed my life-purpose statement on the tombstone, which I look at every day as a reminder.

My transformation in my body is worth its mention. Purpose is not a fancy thought in the head. It is a strong intention that originates from the depths of the heart and soul and translates itself into thoughts and into action through the body. An unfit and weak body cannot execute the grandiosity of purpose. This is what I realised for myself.

Ignoring my body was easy till illness presented itself. My auto-immune condition since childhood had definitely caused a dent in my self-confidence. After numerous doctor consultations, one day I just held my wounded feet in frustration. And it started showing an improvement. I was puzzled, I did not know what was happening. I repeatedly held my feet again and again and my wounds started healing. Upon reflection, I realised that all my body wanted was Love. I had never touched my wounded feet since childhood, as I felt my feet were ugly. My body started responding and I started to care for them. I discovered the magnanimity of the mind-body connection and became a researcher. Today, I love my body and nourish it proactively. My downtime is minimal and I have developed a technique to listen to my body and its needs. We both are friends now and my body partners with me in executing my purpose.

I have been an all-rounder since childhood - arts, languages, singing, spirituality, religious practices, chanting, psychology, dancing, poetry, and drawing have all been inside me. But the *Am I good enough doubt* would never let me acknowledge and embrace myself fully. As I kept offering therapy and then coaching and facilitation to clients, I started meeting numerous corporate folks who were exactly like me. Due to childhood trauma, they had lost their sense of self. They doubted, remained confused, compared, strived hard, prioritised hard work over other things, felt guilty of not giving enough time to family and personal health and stayed in the negative spiral for life. I realised that uplifting such corporate leaders were a cause that made me feel joyous.

Purpose strengthens when the inner sensing meets the outer need. What I was experiencing was an alignment in my wanting to give to the world, with my clients ready to receive what I have to offer, with value and reverence.

This led me to narrow my niche with, "Ambitious leaders who desire to live in balance while chasing success." I clearly understood their pain points, because I was one among them, earlier. Such ambitious leaders could be working in corporate businesses, visionaries or entrepreneurs, social activists, or anyone who identifies themselves as a leader and wants to succeed with balance. I have termed my body of work the **Energy Mastery** process.

Energy is the life force that flows through you to all the activities that you engage in. For me, discovering my purpose was the first step. It is like deciding to play the violin in order to entertain the audience.

First, the instrument needs to be tuned. The player needs to have the right skills, attitude, and body strength to play. With the right tuning, the right music will reach the audience.

I call the process of tuning the Energy Mastery process. This is inspired by ancient Indian wisdom from a model called panchakoshas. To live my life purpose, energy needs to be balanced and mastered in different aspects of life.

Body energy and vitality, emotional energy, thought energy, and energy of your purpose, need to be in the right balance through daily habits so that I stay in alignment with my purpose and what comes through me is aligned action. This will bring fulfillment and joy.

While I discovered this for myself, this became the medium of executing my life purpose. I use this framework in my Leadership Facilitation, coaching and speaking engagements.

When purpose becomes a way of life and it is not a **Doing**, but is embodied by the **Being**. It just flows and that is how it is flowing through me today.

I AM … I AM … I AM …

I AM an embodiment of my purpose and the transformation I wish to see in the Leaders I serve.

I AM extremely clear about my pursuits, the people around me, my clients and life overall. I choose every moment.

I AM a master of my energy and I stand tall. I have a huge reverence for my body.

I AM a healer, I hold special gifts within me, which I have tapped into and offered to the world.

I AM powerful beyond measure and I hold that power with humility.

I joyfully serve humanity through my offerings of leadership facilitation and coaching.

I AM a lifelong learner, I keep learning new modalities to deepen my awareness and self-mastery.

I AM ambitious and I unapologetically strive to enhance my professional accomplishments.

I AM joyous, I live my purpose every minute.

I AM clear about my priorities and choices, and I can assert my boundaries while living my purpose.

Purpose gives meaning to my existence. I love each day because it's a new opportunity to serve. I stand as an inspiration to myself and others who are on this journey of achieving success with balance.

Deepa Mahesh

Founder and CEO of Poorna Wellbeing, Deepa Mahesh is a Leadership Coach and Facilitator. As a Self-Mastery Expert, Deepa facilitates Conscious Leadership Journeys through her coaching, workshops, and training programs.

Majoring in Psychology, armed with a master's in human resource management, she initially worked for some of the top corporations of India including Aditya Birla Group as an HR Leader. In search of her purpose, she quit, to invest time in herself, which finally led to the birth of her entrepreneurial venture, through which she has served thousands of leaders to walk on the path of purpose and achieve success.

Dance and other arts have been her friends since childhood. Her curiosity to explore the mind-body connection led her to exploring expressive arts therapy as her profession and thereafter practicing as an embodiment coach for leaders. As a natural progression, she completed her six years Eurythmy training in 2022. She now holds Eurythmy workshops for adults and teaches the curriculum to primary school students of Kingdom of Childhood, a Waldorf school in Bangalore.

A TEDx Speaker, Mandala Artist and teacher, an Eurythmist, dancer, an embodiment coach, poet and an upcoming author, Deepa balances her life with a myriad of passion projects. She holds Love in her essence and spreads her energy to all those who come in contact with her presence.

Connect with Deepa at https://poornawellbeing.com/.

CHAPTER 8

Well Done on Maximizing Your Talents and Loving Your Being!

Jennifer M. Clarke

Imagine going through life thinking that you did not have any gifts or talents. Imagine having had numerous jobs and careers, but never really knowing your true purpose. "Finding Your Purpose" starts with having the freedom to explore what your gifts and talents could be out of all the vast possibilities, both known and unknown. There are so many opportunities in many different areas that we haven't been educated in and haven't discovered yet. We may not even realize all of our potential, our talents, or our purpose in life. That is until we are educated and begin to experience the numerous possibilities that are available. Often children are told that they should pursue a particular profession in life, often related to their parents' ideals, and aren't given other options. This can become a significant issue, especially if they don't have the innate ability, drive, and discipline to pursue the education needed for the career that was chosen for them.

As a young girl, I would see other children have amazing talents and gifts and I wondered if I had any talents at all. I would then compare myself to them and think that I had no talents and definitely not any that I knew about yet. I hoped that one day I would know what my talents were and be able to excel at them. As I grew up, I would hear about the parable of the talents and I became concerned that I would end up being like the person that had buried their talents. If I had no talents or no apparent talents, then by default they were buried because I didn't even know what mine were or even if I had any at all.

"Finding Your Purpose" starts by taking a look at what you really wanted to have happen by the end of your time here on this Earth. The parable of the talents has pushed me forward through life in recognizing my own talents that I can grow and use to accomplish amazing things. The moral of this parable is to acknowledge your talents and use them to accomplish the things in life you want to do and are called to do, instead of burying them away and hiding them from the world to see and experience. When you know what you want to accomplish and where you want to be in your life, you can work your way backward from your ideal goals. When you know what your victorious finish looks like, then you can choose the best path that can bring you to your ultimate desired accomplishments, and potentially more than you ever could have imagined!

I was directed from childhood until I was a young adult to go into the medical field, without being allowed to explore any other possibilities for a career. I put my whole heart into the health and wellness field for many years, which created amazing results for my clients. The health programs I created were highly effective because I truly care about my clients and want them to have perfect health. Even with these successful results, I still didn't think that I was maximizing my gifts and talents. This career path had many great opportunities, but it always felt as though I was not living up to my full potential in a field in which I could truly excel. It seemed more like a safe career path that I was truly good at doing, but not the path that would be most fulfilling.

There was a certain level of satisfaction when seeing others receive a solution to their health issues. However, I sensed there was something more that I was supposed to be doing that would maximize my gifts and talents. My husband knew exactly what he was meant to do in life within six months of the two of us being married. I was 20 and he was 22 years old when he knew what his purpose was in life. We were taking a biblically based marriage course when my husband had a life-changing experience and sensed that he was meant to save hurting and broken marriages. He became laser-focused on pursuing this path by completing a master's degree in clinical psychology. He did this while we were raising our children, volunteering many hours each week, and working full-time in the health field. We were also teaching the marriage course, as volunteers, that had been so profoundly impactful on both of our lives. This marriage course was even more impactful in my husband's life, as he found his life's purpose while we took it and taught it to other married couples. When my husband discovered that saving marriages was his "calling" in life, I had just assumed his life's purpose was mine, as well. This was because we were married and if his calling was to be helping marriages, I assumed this was a calling for both of us.

Over the last 27 years, we taught a biblically based marriage course and implemented the principles into our personal and professional lives. My husband not only discovered his life's purpose, but when he graduated, became registered, and opened up his counseling practice; he found out that saving marriages was also his gift and talent, which made him very successful at it. My husband hadn't promoted his counseling practice when he started. Nobody would have known that his specialty was counseling married couples. Some married couples who were hurting from infidelity and separation would receive four counseling sessions from my husband and then they would move back in together and renew their vows. The results consistently continued, where his clients would see miraculous results in four sessions, on average, over a variety of issues that for most people are usually hard to overcome. I continued to think that this was the purpose and calling in life for both of us. When we taught the marriage course or counseled together, we could see how we were both impacting married couples in a positive, life-changing way. Even with these amazing transformations, I still didn't know if my husband's purpose and calling were my primary purpose and calling, as well.

Many countless days were focused on taking care of our amazing children and home, which was a large part of our purpose in life. Raising children is a huge part of our life's purpose. We also served other families and children, while raising our own. We were continually volunteering by serving married couples, children, youth, and adults. These activities kept me busy and I continued to put off the question of my life purpose within my own career. The daily tasks of taking care of our children, volunteering, and working kept my mind focused on keeping everything running smoothly, rather than on whether I was truly pursuing my purpose. I knew that I was meant to do something great in my purposeful career path, but for so long I would be influenced by other people's dreams and their projected purpose for me for my own life.

The day that I received a powerful blessing from my father, my life as I knew it changed forever. I will save the details of this blessing for another book that I will write in the future. I found one of my main purposes in life was to become a Business Coach, releasing the gifts, callings, and treasures that I have inside of me. The pivotal experiences in my life that guided me to become a Business Coach are my public speaking experiences, my work with people one-on-one within the health and wellness field, marriage counseling, and financial planning. I also built and helped others build six and seven-figure businesses and had real estate investments that have contributed to being a Business Coach who can coach clients in almost any area or niche. None of this would have been possible without my amazing husband who supported me as I took time off work to pursue my educational goals.

I have always excelled at public speaking. I remember in high school when my parents and teachers would tell me I had a gift for public speaking and that I should join debate clubs. I won awards because of my gift of public speaking. Over the years, this led to my ability to give keynote speeches, along with hosting webinars, seminars, summits, live events, retreats, and workshops. I have spoken to audiences with men, women, children, teens, and young adults. These experiences strengthened my ability to communicate effectively and learn skills that are useful to motivate people.

I've been a volunteer in numerous charitable areas. Donating thousands of hours of my time, energy, efforts, and talents to serve many people in various capacities. Quite often, I would surprise myself because I would be able to do so many things that didn't come easily and naturally to me. However, because I saw a need and wanted to serve others, the gifts and talents were found when I looked deep and just took action and did what needed to be done. For instance, people would think that I had the gift of administration because I organized so many events such as free children's and teen's camps, marriage and health retreats, and many live events. However, organizing and administrative work doesn't come easily to me. It takes a lot of those talents to pull off numerous events. Perhaps if I had an overly analytical and administrative personality type, it could have hindered me from actually taking action. I think because I'm a person who takes action, I've had to have other talents rise up in my areas of weakness to be able to complete the organizing of events.

Having knowledge and experience in the health and wellness field, marriage coaching, financial planning, and many other areas have all resulted in becoming a Business Coach who can coach my clients toward success in almost any area of business or specific niche. Working with people one-on-one, whether it was within the health field, through marriage coaching with my husband, or helping people with their financial planning helped me to be able to relate to my clients' areas of expertise. My background has given me the skills to know how to create a business plan for my clients that shows them how to enroll clients into their business, quickly.

Partnering with people who now have six or seven-figure businesses has expanded my expertise on how to start a business, find clients, and generate a steady income. People who earn that level of income start to think differently about their own lives and beliefs. It changes the way they view money, opportunities, and even themselves. The most successful clients make decisions quickly and implement the action steps needed to succeed, immediately. Studies have shown that quick decision makers are the most successful in life and I've seen this to be true when coaching my own clients. Making quick decisions and implementing them by taking immediate action is the fastest path to success. This is a mindset that I encourage each of my clients to have and I reward them when they make quick decisions. This is because I know from my experience, having seen it numerous times, that they will be my most successful clients.

As a Business Coach, knowing when to challenge a client versus knowing when to encourage a client is of great importance. Public speaking, working one-on-one with many clients over the years, and coaching business owners to launch, grow, and scale their businesses have shown me how delicate the balance is between challenging and encouraging entrepreneurs. If you only challenge someone, they may not have the motivation to keep building their business up. If you only encourage them, they may not build their business with the level of urgency and drive that they need to get to the next level. Bringing a balance between challenge and encouragement will provide an opportunity for the business owner to achieve their ultimate goals when they implement the action steps that are required to succeed.

All of these experiences I had throughout my life, made me realize some key things about myself and my own gifts for coaching. Helping others find their passions and create a business from it brings a lot of joy to my life. It activates all of the skills I excel in the most and have developed in all the careers and titles I've held, with the plethora of experiences that I have been through. Coaching my clients to help them find their gifts, talents, and treasures, find their calling, and be financially rewarded for making an impact in the world, brings me a lot of fulfillment.

I believe that finding your purpose isn't about one subject, niche, career, or area of focus. It is a combination of being in the position of impacting the next generation, a member of your family, a contributing member of your community, and being a positive influence on each life you come into contact with. It's not one thing that we do in life, it's the multitude of things that we do that make up our entire lives and reveal our purpose in this life. It's releasing every gift, talent, and treasure that we have into this world. It's embracing the pressure that is placed upon our weaknesses to bring out even more talents, gifts, and treasures that we didn't even know that we had until the pressure was applied, similar to how a diamond is created. There is a balance between not putting too much stress on yourself versus putting too little. Finding your purpose is looking for ways that you can impact people for the better on the smaller scales and larger stages of life.

"Finding Your Purpose" is the small details of smiling, encouraging, and appreciating the people in your life, even if it's just for a short moment in time. Your purpose could be to hold your baby all day even when you're exhausted and haven't had a chance to take a shower or do laundry. Your purpose in life could be to just exist because it allows others to live life to the full, just knowing that you're here with them on this earth. Your purpose could be found in knowing that you have value just because you are a human being. Knowing that your value is the same whether you're performing at your peak or even if you can't get off the couch because of a significant loss in your life.

Your value is based on who you are and not what you do. This is why we are called Human "Beings" and not Human "Doings," as my husband shared with me early on in our marriage, over 27 years ago. Why do we always think that "Finding Our Purpose" means that we are "doing" something? What if "Finding Our Purpose" partly means finding out who we truly are and loving everything about ourselves: the good, the bad, the ugly, and every single weakness that we have? What if someone put their arm around you and said how much they loved each and every one of your weaknesses and named them one by one? Would this be a shock to what you believe about how we are supposed to show up in the world, how we are conditioned to be in this world, and what we are told to value in this world? What if discovering what all of your weaknesses are is part of your purpose in this life and showing the world how weak you truly are in those areas while still making an impact for good even if your weaknesses become known? What if everything that we know and that we've been conditioned to believe is actually the opposite of our purpose?

Our weaknesses can be the greatest power that we have on this earth. If anything good comes from our weaknesses, wouldn't that be called a miracle? What if our purpose on this earth is to be a conduit for miracles? What if we could accomplish so much more by knowing, acknowledging, and leaning into our weaknesses than we ever could by utilizing our strengths? What if the real power is hidden in our weaknesses and we've missed everything that we were actually meant to do in this world?

What if the smallest things in this world have the greatest power? I think our weaknesses are like the atom. The greatest amount of power has come from an atom. If we can harness the energy that is found in our weaknesses and do the impossible, making all things possible, including miracles, then we have stepped into a realm of unlimited, infinite possibilities. There are things that we think we could never do with our own innate natural gifts and talents; however, if the impossible is accomplished and made possible then how much more significant would it be to see it happen?

Your weaknesses have a purpose and each one of them can be loved. Maybe your weaknesses aren't loved by you or those closest to you, as they are viewed as something that is negative. However, having weaknesses could become your superpower in accomplishing your purpose in this life. What are the weaknesses that you have, can you list them off one by one? Each and every one of those weaknesses has a purpose in this life just as much as your strengths. Your weaknesses are part of making you a unique human being on this earth, just as much as your strengths do. How will you harness your weaknesses to make them your greatest potential power to do good in this world and accomplish your purpose in this life?

Instead of just looking at our strengths, our gifts, our talents, our accomplishments, and all of the doings that we have done in our life.

Let's instead take a really hard look at our weaknesses and dive deep into the power that they potentially have to bring healing and impact for the good toward ourselves and toward others in our lives and potentially throughout the world. What if we had groups of people who gathered together to share their weaknesses with each other and celebrated and rejoiced in them? Is this concept counter-cultural and does it go against everything that we have been raised to believe and to celebrate and rejoice in?

You are invited to celebrate your weaknesses, so you can discover and explore how your weaknesses are part of your life's purpose. I encourage you to gather with your closest and most supportive friends and family to share what your weaknesses are with them and how they are part of your purpose in life. You could then celebrate your weaknesses and choose to love them. Letting go of all pride, pretentiousness, arrogance, and "imposter syndrome." Celebrating the real value of your weakness and the power that is contained in these miracle-making aspects of yourself. Let's really love our weaknesses and love ourselves, so we can love others well, as we love ourselves. Then let's acknowledge and believe that a big part of our intrinsic value is found in our weaknesses and that we have infinite value by just breathing and by just being a Human Being.

Jen M. Clarke

Jen M. Clarke has been a highly successful Business Coach to clients from all over the world.

Jen is known for her expertise in helping Entrepreneurs, Coaches, Consultants, and Business Owners enroll high-ticket, high-paying clients within a day to a few weeks, on average! Jen M. Clarke has many years of experience building 6 and 7-figure businesses in various fields including financial planning, health and wellness, and retreats. Jen has also worked for not-for-profit charities and has organized events, retreats, and conferences. She has established herself as a leading authority as a Business Coach. Jen M. Clarke specializes in helping her clients attract and enroll high-ticket clients. She has developed a proven method and step-by-step formula that coaches entrepreneurs to position themselves as the authority and experts in their field. Jen coaches her clients to communicate in a way that is highly effective to build their businesses very quickly when it's implemented. Jen is known for her customized, engaging, and empowering Business Coaching. Jen is a speaker and has delivered keynote speeches at live events, retreats, workshops, seminars, conferences, and many other types of events, both in-person and online. Jen M. Clarke has a commitment to excellence in helping her clients succeed, so they can reach their full potential! Jen's ultimate vision is for her and her clients to have a significant impact in this world to create a powerful Legacy!

Connect with Jen M. Clarke at https://coachjenclarke.com.

CHAPTER 9

Purpose Is the Source of Prosperity

Julie Steelman

This chapter is dedicated to my father who taught me how
to think, how to be of service to others, and how
to thrive financially.

In my role as an income acceleration coach and money mindset mentor, I have come to understand that purpose is not a fixed concept. It's a dynamic force that weaves through the tapestry of our lives, connecting various experiences, talents, and choices. This belief finds its roots in the earliest memories of my childhood, which set me on a lifelong journey toward discovering the true essence of purpose.

At the tender age of six, my family and I used to gather to watch Mutual of Omaha's Wild Kingdom every Sunday evening. Those hours spent in front of the television were like a portal to a magical world filled with giraffes, lions, elephants, and rhinos. It was during these moments that I felt a profound calling, an undeniable impulse that I couldn't ignore.

The dream that took shape within me during those evenings was crystal clear: I had to visit Africa before I died. It was an intense impulse of crystal-clear clarity, there was no questioning it. It was just so.

It transcended rationality for a young child. But as I looked around at my family, especially my three older brothers, I couldn't help but think, "My parents will never let me go to Africa."

This realization marked a pivotal moment, one where I understood that I would need to carve my own path to financial independence to turn this dream into reality. It might seem unusual for a child to have such thoughts, but it was my truth.

This experience planted the seed of purpose in my life. There was something propelling me forward, something profoundly significant, and I couldn't dismiss it. As the years flowed by, I journeyed through high school and later enrolled in fashion merchandising school.

The fashion industry predominantly thrived in New York City, a place that felt like the polar opposite of where I wanted to live. That's when I knew I needed to attend a traditional four-year college.

I moved to Los Angeles after completing my four-year college degree, majoring in marketing and advertising, and adding a double major in business administration, economics, and marketing and advertising.

Fast forward to my young adult years, and I found myself navigating the corporate world. I had chosen a different path than my childhood dreams of fashion design, influenced by my father that climbing the corporate ladder was the surest route to financial success. Yet, from the moment I set foot in that corporate office, a thought echoed in my mind: "I need to earn my way out of here, fast."

That was when I realized there was this wise voice deep inside that knew better. It was this persistent impulse that kept whispering of a different life, a life more aligned with adventure and authenticity. I felt a greater pull towards a life of globetrotting, board shorts, and flip-flops, rather than the corporate boardroom.

It was as if an inner whisper was tempting me to see things differently, to want more than what society said I should want. It was teasing me and taunting me with ideas of how things could be if only I would follow its beaconing light down a path I couldn't yet know. This feeling of curiosity rose up inside of me, wondering what I actually could become were I to follow such a whisper that was filled with unknown possibilities.

As I labored in the corporate world, selling advertising and later venturing into the realm of online advertising, I began to wonder about the true essence of my purpose. It was 1995, and we were on the brink of the internet revolution. I found myself managing the sales team for a magazine that bundled AOL discs into its pages, a seemingly trivial task at the time.

However, destiny had other plans. As destiny would have it, a 19-year-old video gamer, who spent his days hacking the world wide web, before anyone knew it existed, joined our team as a champion of the future. Our office was at capacity so he moved into my roomy corner office. At first, I didn't take him seriously at all. I could not see what this internet thing would ever do for us. And then one day, my perspective shifted.

Spending time with this young visionary, I began to realize that the internet was more than a passing fad; it was a means of empowering consumers. The impulse to contribute to this transformation stirred me, and I recognized that I had the capacity to offer solutions to well-known brands, helping them thrive in this new digital landscape.

It hit me like a ton of bricks that I had something to say about this new powerful resource. I understood how to help clients grasp it and adopt it as part of their brand strategy. Ideas for creating groundbreaking presentations flooded my mind. And they were radical for the times. But these impulses defied corporate norms and kept urging me to take risks, make bold moves, and have brave conversations with clients in a new way because I had found a purpose for my job.

It was during this phase that I realized we were in the process of returning power to consumers through the launch of the internet. This realization transformed my perspective and urged me to speak out. It was as if my purpose was beckoning me, guiding me towards a new path. I realized I had something to say.

As I continued to climb the corporate ladder, getting asked to speak on more and more stages, since I had a gift for articulating the complex, I started to excel in my role. One of the gifts purpose gave me was the ability to share a big message on important stages. Had I not followed those guiding impulses, I would never have discovered this about myself.

As I continued to listen to this inner impulse, I started to make big money. Purpose, I found, is the source of prosperity. Purpose became the driving force behind my success, propelling me to go above and beyond to solve customer problems, share my insights, and, ultimately, earn a substantial income. By listening to my inner callings, taking risks, and following my instincts, even when they contradicted corporate norms, I was able to attain financial success. Purpose ignites the fire of prosperity within.

During my years as a regional sales manager at Microsoft, everything seemed picture-perfect. I had the accolades, the shiny toys, and the financial security that many aspire to. On paper, it looked like

I had it all figured out. But sometimes, life has a way of delivering a wake-up call when you least expect it.

It all happened during one particular board meeting that changed the trajectory of my life. I vividly remember the VP discussing the need to "delete" team members as if they were mere disposable assets. At that moment, it hit me like a ton of bricks – if they saw people that way, then I, too, was replaceable. That realization hit me like a lightning bolt, and I knew I needed to rediscover what truly mattered to me.

So, without hesitation, I fled that suffocating boardroom and headed home. My gut told me I needed to reconnect with something far more important than climbing the corporate ladder. It was in that frantic moment that I picked up the phone and called my trusty travel buddy. Together, we booked a spontaneous scuba diving trip, a desperate escape from the chaos of my corporate career.

Little did I know that this impulsive decision would lead me to an extraordinary encounter – the love of my life, my beloved late husband. Our connection was instant, and from the moment we met, we were inseparable. It was as if the thread of purpose had woven our lives together by magic. It's a beautiful reminder that purpose is always conspiring on our behalf, designing pivotal moments that we might never have experienced if we hadn't followed that inner thread.

Ultimately, at the age of 47, I realized my dream of earning my way out of corporate America. My late husband and I relocated to Hawaii, but the impulse to visit Africa still lingered. It was a dream I couldn't let go of.

Over the years, I have visited Africa 14 times, exploring nine different countries on the continent. This may seem unrelated to purpose, but it's a testament to the power of listening to your inner callings. I have become an internationally award-winning wildlife photographer because I deeply care about the animals and the planet.

What I have come to understand is that purpose is multifaceted. My purpose isn't solely about visiting Africa or being a wildlife photographer; it's twofold. It's about being an advocate for animals and empowering women to achieve financial security, enabling them to pursue their dreams.

Remember that purpose encompasses more than just money and material success. It includes generosity, passion, well-being, and empowerment. It's the secret ingredient that adds richness and meaning to your life.

There's a common misconception about purpose—that it can be distilled into a single, easily defined word or phrase. However, my life journey has taught me that purpose is far more intricate than that. It's not just about what your purpose is; it's also about what you bring into the world and how you nurture it.

Imagine the spark of purpose as a tiny but radiant ember glowing within the depths of your soul. It's like a distant star in the night sky, faint yet steadfast, guiding you through life's vast expanse. This cosmic spark has a magnetic quality, pulling you toward your unique journey and the fulfillment of your deepest desires. Just as a lighthouse beacon cuts through the darkness, your purpose serves as your guiding light, illuminating the way forward.

This spark can be thought of as a hidden treasure buried deep within the forest of your being. It's the elusive, shimmering gem that has been waiting patiently for you to discover it. Much like a curious archaeologist, you embark on an inner excavation, digging through layers of experiences and self-discovery to unearth this precious jewel.

And when you finally hold it in your hands, you realize that it's not just a gem but a multifaceted diamond of immense value. This diamond is your purpose, and its brilliance can light up your life and the lives of those around you.

We tend to view purpose as a solitary, easily identifiable word or statement. Nevertheless, it's more about the energy it embodies. I began to understand that my purpose wasn't confined to one thing; it was a thread that wove through my life, connecting various experiences and choices. Purpose is a path, not a thing.

Purpose is a multifaceted and intricate concept, like a tapestry woven from the threads of our experiences, passions, talents, and values. It's not a one-size-fits-all notion. It evolves over time, shaped by the various experiences of our lives. This complexity arises from the pull of our inner desires and the external world, the intersection of our personal aspirations with our assumed role as defined by society.

Many people equate purpose solely with their career or ambition, but its complexity extends far beyond these realms. It encompasses not only what we do for a living but also how we relate to others, how we contribute to our communities, and how we seek personal growth and fulfillment. Purpose is the driving force behind our actions, guiding us in our pursuit of meaningful connections, well-being, and a sense of belonging. It challenges us to explore the depths of our values, pushing us to align our actions with what truly matters to us.

One of the most intriguing aspects of purpose is its ever-evolving nature. It's not a static destination but an evolutionary journey, adapting as we grow, learn, and change. What we perceive as our purpose today may transform as we gain new insights, face different life stages, or encounter unexpected challenges. True purpose invites us to be flexible and open-minded in our pursuit of it, allowing us to embrace the facets of our own unique life tapestry.

To truly grasp the profound interplay between purpose and prosperity, it's vital to understand that purpose is not a separate idea from the path to financial well-being; instead, it's the driving force behind it. When you're aligned with your purpose, you're more likely to excel in your chosen endeavors because you're tapping into a deep well of motivation and passion. It's like having a limitless reservoir of energy that propels you forward, enabling you to overcome challenges, persevere through setbacks, and consistently deliver your best work. In this way, purpose becomes the catalyst for achieving financial success, as it becomes the source of your determination and resilience.

Furthermore, purpose directs your focus toward creating value for others. When your actions are driven by a sense of purpose, you naturally seek to make a meaningful impact in the lives of those you serve. This genuine desire to contribute to the well-being of others often leads to greater financial rewards, as people are more inclined to support and invest in individuals and businesses that are aligned with a higher mission.

Purpose-driven professionals and entrepreneurs find that their customers or clients are not merely transactions but part of a broader community connected by a shared vision. This sense of purpose-driven connection can result in increased customer loyalty and a thriving network, which are valuable assets in any financial journey.

Additionally, purpose has a profound effect on your mindset and decision-making when it comes to financial matters. It encourages a long-term perspective, emphasizing sustainable wealth-building rather than quick gains.

Purpose-driven individuals tend to make more deliberate and responsible financial choices, prioritizing investments that align with their values and long-term goals. They're less likely to succumb to impulsive spending or excessive risk-taking, which can lead to financial instability.

Instead, they approach financial decisions with a clear sense of purpose, aiming for financial security and freedom that supports their mission and allows them to give back to causes they care about.

Lastly, purpose fosters a holistic view of prosperity that extends beyond financial wealth. It encompasses well-being in all aspects of life, including physical health, mental and emotional balance, and meaningful relationships.

A sense of purpose provides the motivation to maintain a healthy work-life balance, prioritize self-care, and nurture relationships with loved ones. This holistic approach to prosperity ensures that financial success is not pursued at the expense of overall well-being but is harmoniously integrated into a fulfilling and purpose-driven life.

In essence, purpose and prosperity are intricately woven together, with purpose serving as the catalyst, compass, and sustenance on the journey to financial well-being. By recognizing the profound connection between these two elements and actively cultivating a sense of purpose in your endeavors, you empower yourself to not only achieve success but also experience a deeper and more meaningful form of prosperity that enriches every facet of your life.

It's common that most of us spend countless hours worrying and wondering about our purpose when, in reality, it's already within us, just waiting to be acknowledged. Purpose is not an elusive treasure hidden in the depths of the unknown; it's a vibrant, living energy that resides in everyone's soul. Rather than searching endlessly outside of ourselves to find our elusive purpose, it's much wiser to turn our gaze inward.

Imagine all the time and energy wasted on this quest for external validation of purpose, seeking approval from others, or trying to fit into predefined roles. When the truth is, the very essence of what we seek is already a part of us. Purpose isn't something to be found; it's something to be recognized, nurtured, and allowed to flourish. It's those small, everyday moments when your heart sings with joy or you feel an undeniable pull toward something; that's your purpose calling to you.

Embracing the fact that purpose is an innate part of your being is liberating. It shifts the focus from seeking validation to self-discovery. By listening to your inner impulses and nurturing the passions that stir your soul, you can unlock the boundless potential of your purpose. It's a journey of self-acceptance, trust, and empowerment, ultimately leading to a life of profound meaning and fulfillment.

Purpose involves aligning with that deeper, wider universal intelligence. It's about opening yourself up to synchronize with the universe's callings for what you need.

On this path, you'll inevitably encounter obstacles and challenges. However, it's through these challenges that you evolve, adapt, and become more resilient. Your purpose isn't just about circumventing obstacles; it's about transcending them.

Rather than seeking a fixed answer to the question of your purpose, embrace the lifelong quest. Your purpose will reveal itself as you listen to those impulses and follow your heart. By following your purpose, you'll cultivate profound self-trust and confidence. It's a journey that demands audacity and the willingness to step into the unknown.

Listening to your purpose might lead others to label you as a maverick, a rebel, or a troublemaker. Yet, these are often the labels worn by those who dared to listen and follow their unique calling.

In the grand scheme of things, purpose is the driving force propelling us forward in life. It encompasses more than mere financial wealth; it encompasses generosity, passion, well-being, and empowerment.

Purpose isn't a fixed point; it's a journey of self-discovery and sharing your best self with others.

I urge you to stop searching for your purpose in the conventional sense. Instead, concentrate on living your impulses, and your passions. Embrace what truly matters to you and be willing to heed that audacious call. It's within these audacious calls that you'll uncover the authentic essence of your purpose.

Remember that the beauty of the journey lies in living in the questions rather than seeking concrete answers. By remaining curious and open to the unknown, we allow our purpose to reveal itself organically.

Julie Steelman

As a prominent Money Mindset Expert and Income Accelerator Coach for professional and entrepreneurial women, Julie Steelman is renowned for her unwavering commitment to helping entrepreneurial women secure their financial futures. With an illustrious career spanning years of dedication, Julie has become a respected authority in the field of feminine prosperity, recognized for her expertise in guiding women through transformative financial journeys.

With a profound understanding of the unique challenges that midlife professional women face, Julie has developed a proven strategy for getting her clients potent results. She has emerged as a thought leader who empowers her clients to take charge of their financial destinies. Her approach combines strategic insight with a deep understanding of personal empowerment, setting her apart as a visionary in the realm of financial security.

Julie's transformative coaching methodologies have helped countless women triple their income, navigate midlife transitions, and create lasting financial stability. Through her dynamic seminars, masterclasses, and personalized coaching sessions, she provides tangible, actionable strategies that lead to tangible results.

Connect with Julie at https://www.juliesteelman.com.

CHAPTER 10

Life by Design, Not by Default

Karsta Marie Hurd

For my babies. My one true purpose.

It was my third year of university; that time when everyone was making and finalizing the big decisions. Except me, I had no idea. Actually, I had ideas, they just didn't excite me. They were ... fine.

One day, standing in my apartment, I had a vision of myself after college. I was an extremely successful international businesswoman. I envisioned myself flying first class or on private jets, wearing designer clothes. The details of what I saw were fascinating. More powerful than what I saw, though, was what I felt - confident, successful, free. To this day, anytime I tell the story, I get chills. It was so exhilarating!

I quickly ran to the registrar and enrolled in Accounting 101. I would finish the Spanish major I had been working toward and add a business degree. That moment was the first time in my life that I had ever actually made my own plan for the future. I was excited and proud.

By the end of the semester it was abundantly clear that I was not business minded. Adding and subtracting debits and credits - What even?! I barely passed that class (and I'm pretty sure the only reason I did was because I was cleaning the professor's house). With my tail between my legs, I trekked back to the registrar's office. It made more sense to start building something more realistic.

After spending a semester in Spain to finish out my Spanish major, I was to complete my Student Teaching experience the following year - 7th grade Spanish in a small rural town that was an hour away from where I lived. Every day I made the two-hour round trip. Every day I struggled. Finally, with only two weeks left of the year, on a Friday afternoon, after a long talk with my supervising teacher, I called my professor. "What can I do? At this point, I don't want to pursue my teaching license, I just want to be able to graduate in two weeks. Is it possible to step out of my teaching role and just observe and still get credit? Again, I have no intention of getting my license. I just need to be done."

Her response, "Well, I'm not surprised. I knew you were never cut out to be a teacher."

What a punch to the gut.

Ultimately, I would either have to finish student teaching or stay an extra semester, which, according to my parents, wasn't an option.

I graduated college with a degree in Spanish and Secondary education. After twenty-five years in education, I don't mind telling you, I was good at it - really good. But, my professor wasn't entirely wrong. It's not my soul's calling. Teaching comes easily to me, so I endured it, because it made sense, but it doesn't fill my cup.

I was also engaged to my college sweetheart. We planned a beautiful wedding and got married. I started a secure and honorable career. We built a house in the suburbs, got a dog, had two babies, and even got a minivan (which I loved to hate). I had created the stable, normal picket fence life I thought I had missed out on as a child. Everything was what it was supposed to be and it was fine - until it wasn't.

Suddenly, I found myself knocked off my axis and just trying to re-stabilize everything, not only for myself, but for my two small children. The next few years were, for all intents and purposes, survival mode. There wasn't time, nor did I have the energy for any kind of personal growth. I didn't get therapy, I didn't reflect on my areas of improvement. I just got through each day.

Two years after our divorce was final, I was blessed to connect with a new partner. We both had children and exes to navigate, so things moved slowly, VERY slowly. After nine years together we finally decided to blend our families into the same home. Two years later, that relationship ended. I tell you that story because after that relationship, it started to dawn on me that perhaps I had some healing and reflection to do.

I became a teacher because it's all I knew how to do. I got married, because I didn't know what else to do after college. I had babies because that's what married people did. I got into another relationship, because it was convenient, without much thought about what I really wanted or needed from a partner.

I was living my life by default. Whatever was in front of me and was easy, that's what I did.

It was time to start living by *design*.

If you've ever watched any home renovation show, that's what my journey looked like. What started as some redecorating - a new

105

coat of paint and a few small DIY projects, quickly turned into tearing everything down to the studs and starting over. As soon as I started one project, I'd uncover something deeper that needed to be resolved. So, layer by layer, I tore it all down. ALL OF IT.

So began my *anti-me phase*. At the beginning of 2017, I was in extremely good physical shape. I had shorter blonde hair. I was taking care of myself and working a steady full-time job. By 2018, I had dyed my hair dark, stopped working out and eating well and was barely making ends meet working a part-time job as a barista at a local coffee shop. All in protest of who had been in the past. It stood to reason that if who/what I had been in the past wasn't working for me, I must do the opposite of all of that in order to find what does.

After a LONG five years of rebuilding my life, in a way that makes sense for me, I've learned three things that are now critical pieces of my personal development journey. Before I tell you what they are, I want to be clear that these three things are not stand-alone lessons. They work together in tandem and you must give thought to all of them.

Picture a Venn diagram with purpose: happiness, joy, best life … whatever you're striving for in the center. In the three outer, intertwining circles are: clarity, building and maintaining a loving and trusting relationship with yourself and letting go of the badges of honor that you're carrying (a.k.a. victimhood that you're using as excuses). While all three components work together, and each becomes important at different times, I want to start with **clarity**, because without clarity the rest is moot.

Have you ever tried to ask your GPS for directions AWAY from your current location? No. Because it doesn't work that way. You have to input a specific destination. Once you do, you get so much information. Which route is the fastest, which is the longest, which one has detours.

You get estimated arrival times. And, along the way you get updates. "There is an accident ahead, but you are still on the fastest route."

The same phenomenon is true with the Universe and your intuition. Once you know where you want to go, you'll get such clear guidance. Now, I know what you're thinking, "How do I know my destination? Isn't that what I'm trying to figure out?" While you may not have a clear picture yet, there is an easy way to start creating one.

When I had that vision in college of being an international businesswoman, the powerful part wasn't what I saw, it's what I felt. What I didn't know back then was that what I was really craving in my life weren't things or experiences. It was those feelings of independence, freedom, abundance, and confidence.

One of the most powerful and fastest ways we can create happiness or purpose in our lives is to tap into the feelings we expect to experience once we have the things. Instead of, "I'll be happy when I have _____," try asking yourself how you will *feel* when you have it. What does happiness feel like for you? Find that first. For example, maybe you want to make a lot of money, so that you can take all kinds of adventurous vacations. The feeling behind that - adventure. Instead of waiting for the money, start finding small ways you can feel adventure in your life now, while you build your financial abundance.

I didn't have to become a successful international businesswoman, I just needed to find freedom, abundance, and confidence (and a few other feelings I've learned that I want) in my everyday life.

While there are definitely elaborate visualization meditations I've done to help me get that clarity, getting clear on how you want to feel inside your life is as simple as this - every morning when you wake up ask yourself, "How do I want to feel today?"

The second piece to finding clarity is this - when it's not all going the way you want it to, you don't have to burn it to the ground like I did. The *anti-me phase*, while informative, was unnecessary. Sometimes, you just need to take the blinders off, stop focusing on what's not working, look around and see what IS working for you. Had I done that back in 2017, I would've noticed that while I was tired of feeling like a slave to diet culture (the reason I had gotten into such good shape in the first place), working out regularly and eating well did bring with it the power, confidence, and freedom I had wanted before. All I needed to do was notice what was working, and then just tweak what wasn't.

Finding clarity, believe it or not, was the easiest lesson for me. The hardest - learning to trust myself. For much of my life, I sat back quietly and passively doing what everyone else told me to do. I assumed that most people were more knowledgeable than me or, in the case of my family, just simply knew what was best for me. I never learned how to trust myself. This is common for many of us with childhood trauma.

So, I began nurturing a relationship with myself. I treated it like any new relationship. I had to get to know myself again. I had to build trust little by little. Both in terms of trusting that I would take action when necessary and in knowing that whatever guidance my intuition gave me was solid and in alignment with my goals. I had to start small ("what should I have for breakfast" small) and it has taken serious commitment - just like any relationship. I'm happy to report, things are pretty serious between myself and I. When She (my intuition) is showing me something that seems completely crazy, I trust her enough to at least put the option on the table and explore it.

I already mentioned those pesky childhood (and sometimes adulthood) traumas. Not only did they leave me untrusting and untrustworthy of myself, but they became these badges of honor that I wore to protect myself. Actually, they were excuses. But, they came in handy as good reasons not to do things that scared me.

So many times I thought of quitting my job as a teacher and doing something else. Something that would've filled my cup. But, I would always chicken out. "I can't do that because... teaching is a good, stable job / I don't know how to do anything else / I'm a single mom and need a stable job...." I had an arsenal of excuses. I think we all do. In a nutshell, they loosely translate to, "I'm too scared to do that, because I don't feel worthy or capable." And, they usually stem from those pesky traumas I mentioned above.

The most important thing I had to remind myself is this - those things are part of your story, but they do not define you.

Read that again.

Taking off those badges can be tricky and difficult. Some of them have been a huge part of our identity for a long time. All we can do is take them off one at a time. If you can't actually take them off just yet, start reframing them. Instead of, "I can't do that because I'm a single mom." (that was my go-to for a number of years) flip the script. "It's going to be hard because I'm a single mom, but look at all the other things I've done as a single mom." Or, "How can I try to make it work even though I'm a single mom?"

I want to throw one last bonus lesson in here that I've learned - finding your purpose is not a journey with a final destination. It is a never-ending journey. And that's where the beauty lies.

My current season does not look exactly how I thought it would. However, when I think about how I want to feel inside my life, I'm as close as I've ever been. So, I will sit in gratitude and stay focused on the pieces that are working so that I can continue to grow those. In doing that, the pieces that aren't working are going to fall away, creating more room for even more amazing things to appear.

Karsta Marie Hurd

After twenty-five years as a K-12 educator, Karsta Marie Hurd is now a two-time #1 International Best-Selling author, motivational speaker, and Personal Development expert with a passion for empowering others to live a life by design rather than by default. Her signature blend of empathy, compassion, and candor has captivated audiences worldwide, inspiring action and helping clients break free from limiting beliefs. With her relatable and vulnerable style, Karsta shares insights that help people tap into their inner strength and discover their unique gifts. In her free time, you'll find Karsta walking the trails near her home, binging something on Netflix or spending time with her "ride or die" squad.

Connect with Karsta at https://karstamarie.as.me/30minDiscovery.

CHAPTER 11

Destined for More:
Unveiling Your Life's Purpose

Kim Kelley Thompson

Dedicated to my mother and brother who knew they had a higher calling in life but allowed the demons of self-doubt to rob them of experiencing & sharing their gifts with others.

I am here for a purpose and that purpose is to grow into a mountain, not to shrink to a grain of sand. Henceforth will I apply ALL my efforts to become the highest mountain of all and I will strain my potential until it cries for mercy.
~Og Mandino

We are born on purpose with purpose. Discovering that purpose though, can often be challenging simply because it's not something that can be taught. It exists within and is as unique as your fingerprint. It's not necessarily linked to a specific end goal, it's more of an ongoing impact on others. Purpose is your why. Likewise, your why is your purpose. It's what inspires you to take action and it inspires others to take action with you.

I've come to believe, for myself and those I've interviewed over the years, that one's purpose is often realized during the journey, rather than attained at a final destination. It has the ability to fuel your dreams and keep you going regardless of how many obstacles you may face. Which is why your purpose typically has its roots in difficulties you've been through along with the interests and passions you've developed.

Often the setbacks we face in life are actually set ups for what we are meant to do. If you subscribe to the belief that everything in our life benefits us in some way and that our path is designed to help us live to our potential, then it becomes easier to see our purpose. I've found that our purpose stems from either a struggle or challenge we've experienced and conquered or from a version of the person we once were thus enabling us to understand, appreciate and help others through similar issues.

One thing is for certain, the path to purpose will require us to push our limits. To trust our intuition and know we have incredible strengths when we tap into and rely on our higher self. It is then that we are given the ability to see more possibilities. It is in this space that obstacles become opportunities.

This isn't to say that you have to change the world or be the biggest, best, or brightest. It simply means that you can fulfill your purpose by giving attention to your passion.

Purpose and passion are like two sides of the same coin, they both tap into your interests. However, passion is something you tend to do for yourself, while purpose is something you do for others. Often your passions will help you determine and fulfill your purpose. For example, you may be passionate about filmmaking as well as nature, your purpose may be to protect the environment by creating documentaries. If you have a passion for cooking, perhaps your purpose is to bring families together over delicious meals. Your purpose is not necessarily an elaborate, global changing mission, but it will be something that benefits others.

This is why uncovering and honoring your purpose is essential to a well-rounded, meaningful life. But, it can be uncomfortable and therefore remain a bit elusive because it requires us to stretch into a higher version of ourselves and face unknown territory. Your purpose will always be the driving force that keeps you focused on track and on task, pulling you towards a more evolved level of thinking and being.

When purpose is acknowledged and trusted, it becomes an inner guide that drives decisions and leads to life-altering opportunities that can bring incredible benefits to you and those you are put on this planet to serve.

Yet, if we're all born with a purpose, and if that purpose is truly important to life, then why do many people struggle to find their purpose?

Why do we look to others to tell us what we should or could do? How do we not know? If purpose is genuinely a part of us, why is it that we waste years searching for something we have intrinsically?

I believe our environment, family experience and societal norms can cause us to abandon any sense of purpose we may have once felt.

Instead of trusting our own self and our own inner voice, we begin to doubt it. Questioning if it's even valid and doable.

Unfortunately, this is where many people remain, stuck in an abyss of unfulfilled purpose. I do think we know, perhaps at an unconscious level, what our true purpose is in life. I also believe that purpose continues to morph over time, expanding into broader fields simply because, like energy, purpose must express, when held back it can implode.

I knew early on that my purpose was somehow connected to helping people believe in themselves enough to go after their dreams. In college, I received scholarship money for my desire to create informative shows or events that inspired others to pursue their passions. What exactly those shows or events were, remained undefined. I had vague ideas but had difficulty clarifying my vision. I got so caught up in the fact that I wasn't clear that all my energy became focused on this lack of clarity which simply perpetuated the problem.

At the same time, I diminished the strengths and knowledge I did have, thinking there were others who were far more experienced than I. Over the years, I've come to realize that this belief is an all-too-common issue for many people. Hiding behind the dark veil of vagueness or pushing off what we value and desire for fear that we're not enough only keeps us in limbo, never stepping into our potential and never living our purpose. It's far easier to get caught in thoughts such as, "I don't have enough knowledge, experience, time, energy, or information," despite how frustrating and uncomfortable it may be than it is to step forward with faith toward what we truly desire.

Excuses come in a variety of shapes and sizes. The human mind is tricky, it can easily justify our behavior and give us what appears to be a legitimate reason for remaining stuck. But, if we pay close attention to our feelings and listen for inner guidance, we'll soon see that we've simply been protecting ourselves from true growth.

I watched my dad switch careers and do very well in sales, conducting the majority of his business on the golf course. That was enough of a reason for me to abandon what I knew deep down I wanted to do, and choose a career in sales instead. While there were aspects of sales I enjoyed, certainly the money and the time freedom, I often felt like something was missing.

It was like a part of me had been cut off and I felt every bit of it. My heart would literally ache at times. Occasionally, I'd get a glimpse or a memory of that thing I really wanted to do but had pushed aside to pursue a *real* career.

The funny thing about purpose is that it continues to call us. It may start as a feeling that we can't quite identify but we know it's there. We may hear it as a quiet whisper simply asking us to pay attention.

It may feel as though you know there's something missing, something that truly makes you come alive, something that makes your heart sing. It may show up once in a while, or quite frequently. Often it presents itself as an uneasiness. It's as if you're out of alignment.

You may be able to identify it. You may know exactly what your purpose is, yet you hold it at bay, trying to avoid it. Even if you are not quite sure what it is, you may have this feeling inside that you're meant for more.

No matter how much you try to sidestep it, you feel it. It's almost as if you're dying inside and, in a sense, you are. Because that desire, that something is actually your calling in life, it's your purpose. It's been given to you by Spirit and Spirit is always looking to express itself. It does so through us as humans, because that is how it is glorified.

I continued in sales for several years, despite a sadness that would bubble up from the depths of my soul. I'd be in a sales presentation and I get a vision that didn't quite align with what I was doing. I'd have to quickly pull my mind back to be present and focused on my clients. What I did know was that it was my purpose begging me to listen. But that elated feeling of something more would quickly dissipate in a cloud of how. How could I lean into that desire when the money to support my family was right here in front of me?

I believe that each of us has something we are passionate about, something that we enjoy doing so much, that we can completely lose ourselves in it. But then there's that nagging little voice of self-doubt that says things like, "Seriously give it up, how are you going to do that? Really that's been done. You don't have time for that." There's a plethora of excuses to hide behind.

Yet, in our quiet moments, that purpose rises up and stirs our soul, begging us to listen, "I'm still here, don't let me go."

It speaks softly at first, growing a bit louder with each passing year. It may show up as a dull ache, frustration, lethargy, or even sickness. Make no mistake, it will not leave, certainly not without our permission. Yes, it will persist, determined to get our attention, to make us wake up! Until we realize that the pain of not pursuing our purpose is far greater than the fear of doing so.

I find it fascinating this quiet voice that wants so desperately to be heard, that wants to help us fulfill our dream, has so much determination. It will try any means possible to get our attention. Why then, are many of us so stubborn? Why do we try to walk away using excuses couched in reasoning or practicality? If our own inner being has such tenacity, why then, wouldn't we?

When you know your purpose, you know what you need to, and must do. You no longer look to others to help determine your course in life, instead, you begin to trust yourself and your emotions. You view your experiences as lessons designed to uncover your purpose.

I visited my purpose every once in a while, unpacking it like it was an old toy from childhood. But, somehow, somewhere I bought into the belief that it was safer to take the well-worn path rather than create my own. Perhaps, because no one in my family knew their purpose or if they did, they certainly kept it well hidden.

Purpose though, will not die, it can't. Like our soul, it is designed to live and evolve and it does so through us. Mine would be no exception, it would find its way to the surface no matter which path it had to create. It was determined to be expressed. I finally acknowledged it, but it took me down a path I never expected.

After a 20-year marriage, I found myself divorced and raising four children on my own. We had lost our business. My then ex-husband was out of work and we were on the verge of losing our home. This was certainly not the vision I intended for my life.

In order to keep a roof over our heads and food on the table, I had to go back to work. The only issue, I had been a stay-at-home mom for 12 years. The demons of self-doubt started to take hold and my confidence in myself and my ability to trust was slowly crumbling. I had my own business before I started raising my family. How would I start that again? I didn't have the time to develop a business. But, I needed to get out of the hole we were in fast!

But purpose doesn't die and Spirit always has a plan and I followed it, reluctantly. At the time, there was a grocery store strike happening. Here I was, a magna cum laude graduate and former business owner checking groceries. Looking back now, I can say it was perfect for me at the time. No stress, decent pay and I was home when my children returned from school. I worked every overtime shift I could in order to pay off debt and take my family on a vacation to help ease the pain and trauma of divorce.

A few months later, after brushing my bruised ego aside, I landed a sales position that afforded me the ability to keep my children in the same school district and neighborhood and gave me some flexibility.

That sales position was a huge blessing, it brought me back to visioning and goal setting, passion and purpose. I know we have the ability to create the life we desire. I also know that we are not given desires without the ability to bring them to fruition, whether or not we choose to is up to us. Granted, it may not always come about in the exact way we think it will. There may be various iterations, but I do know that achieving our desires often calls for a deep dive into self. It requires us to push past the ego, limiting beliefs, or the mental games we play that keep us living small.

I'm thankful for that sales position, as it forced me to face my internal fears and doubts and start my own business again.

Except, that dang lack of clarity reared its head once more. While I knew that I was done building someone else's business and I knew I wanted to be at home with my children, I didn't know how I was going to do that. What I did have and what I chose to focus on, was the memory of the purpose I had abandoned years before. This time though, it was backed by a motive stronger than any excuse my mind could throw at me, four to be exact – my children.

My desire to inspire and help others to pursue their passions led me to create an online publication for the hospitality industry which blended my sales experience with my personal development training. There was a slight problem though, I had no idea how to create an online publication. Heck, at the time, I was lucky to add an attachment to an email. But what I learned is that the how never matters. It's desire that drives us to action and with action comes clarity. The how will always present itself, but you must step out in action first.

I created that online publication along with a website. That magazine attracted advertising dollars from top hotel brands and helped me transition full-time into my own business. It also led to the development of two additional businesses – my event production company and, as an offshoot of that, my content development company for the hospitality industry.

That one idea of starting the publication led to three different income sources. Ultimately my coaching and speaking business brought me back to the original purpose I had tried to silence many times over the years.

I believe we have all been given unique talents and abilities along with desires that we absolutely can create, but without action, they become like unused muscle and atrophy. Only through action can we gain the clarity that enables us to see the patterns and habits that we've allowed to dictate our lives. When we raise our standards and change our beliefs, we elevate our behavior. We are then able to take the focused, committed action that purpose is calling us to take.

What I've come to realize is that there is an immense power in purpose, that, when acknowledged, has the ability to create wonders. The power of purpose is similar to the energy of focused light. Diffused light has little use, but when its energy is concentrated, as through a magnifying glass, that same light can set fire to paper. Focus its energy even more, as with a laser beam, and it has the power to cut through steel. A clear sense of purpose enables you to focus your energy and efforts, compelling you to take risks and push forward regardless of the odds or obstacles.

Your purpose is connected to your desires and fueled by your passions. I'm convinced that just in the very nature of being born, we have a responsibility to ourselves, to Spirit, and to others to pursue our purpose. Uncovering and living your purpose starts by first, acknowledging that you have a purpose, a calling in life waiting and wanting to express through you.

Next, believe that it is possible for you. This may mean squashing those subconscious patterns that try to interrupt your efforts, that annoying mental chatter. We silence those by facing them head-on, acknowledging them, and asking ourselves if these beliefs are true or helpful and if they are still serving us. If not, then it's time to let them go and form a new subconscious pattern, which happens through awareness and repetition.

Finally, begin stepping out in faith by taking action, even if it's imperfect action or baby steps. Faith is always rewarded and action always creates clarity.

Know this, you have innate talents and gifts you are meant to live and share with the world, and just as sure as you were given those gifts, you were also given the ability to bring them to life.

We all come into this world with a purpose. While the path to uncovering and pursuing it may seem challenging, it will be the greatest gift you can give yourself and others.

Kim Kelley Thompson

Kim Kelley Thompson is a business and high-performance coach who provides entrepreneurs with the strategies and support they need to turn their business dreams into reality.

Kim stresses practical application, not theory, teaching new and struggling entrepreneurs the same tools and techniques that enabled her to build a thriving production company and online publication attracting advertisers such as Marriott and Hilton Hotels.

Having raised four children by herself, while managing a multimillion-dollar event company and starting her own business, Kim is known for simplifying the process of business building.

She takes an inside-out approach to her teaching, focusing on both the mental and practical steps that build momentum in business. She is a firm believer that personal development and business development go hand-in-hand.

Kim believes that we all have unique talents and abilities along with desires that we absolutely can achieve once we know the steps to take. Desire drives action and action creates clarity. Her work helps people clarify their ideas and create the action steps to achieve them.

Kim is blessed to be a mom, speaker, author, and founder of the Successful Entrepreneurs Association, a networking and mentorship community for entrepreneurs and the Shift or Get Off the Pot podcast.

Connect with Kim at https://calendly.com/kimkthompson/30.

CHAPTER 12

Blossom in the Storm

Kohila Sivas

This chapter is dedicated to all those who have faced darkness and emerged stronger. It is a tribute to the resilience of the human spirit and the transformative power of embracing adversity. This chapter is lovingly dedicated to my son, who stood by me with unwavering support and shared his youthful wisdom. Your presence and encouragement have been a source of strength, reminding me that wisdom knows no age. This chapter is a heartfelt dedication to myself, a reflection of the journey I undertook to learn the profound lessons of self-respect and self-love.

---

nside that chamber, with its stark white walls, I felt suspended. Time seemed to hang motionless. The only disruption to the silence was a steady pulsing beep. It was that sound that stirred me.

I was in a bed, but I could not move. A hospital. I tried to contemplate the sequence of events that brought me here.

It was a narrative filled with heartache. Trials that were beyond what any child should experience. I was just thirteen, but my life was already a string of events that were like heavy anchors.

My earliest memories were set against a backdrop of gunfire, explosions, and helicopters. The haunting sounds of civil war in my homeland of Sri Lanka. Where children once innocently played, now lay the somber shadows of death. Days that should have been filled with laughter and learning were overshadowed by the dread of violence and the need to survive.

I recalled dark nights with my family huddled together in our bunker. Outside, the sounds of conflict raged, while my grandfather would smile and weave happy tales in his attempt to shelter us. Our hearts raced with fear.

Faced with this chaos, my parents made the necessary decision to flee our homeland in search of sanctuary. This wasn't just changing landscapes; it was a shift into an alien world filled with unfamiliar tongues, bitter cold temperatures, and a culture vastly different from ours. Each day was a balancing act, trying to meld our past with this new present.

I recall my first day at school in Canada, where everything was foreign. It was a place where my very existence seemed to clash with the norm. The weight of my differences and the chasm of isolation opened further. The language barrier was a towering wall, and my parents were powerless.

Amid these external challenges, I took an inward step that further isolated me. I silenced myself. The lively, expressive little girl became a shadow. Observing, but never truly participating.

And then came the sad news of my grandparents' deaths. I longed for my grandmother's embrace and my grandfather's kindness. It was heartbreak felt even deeper because I would never say my last goodbyes.

My father struggled badly and fell into addiction. His business had been burned, and he was in a land where he had no identity. He sought solace in alcohol. His struggles spilled over, darkening our lives with a cycle of violence. My mother was powerless, caught in the cycle, seemingly blind.

Then came an act of treachery, one that left an indelible mark not only on my flesh but seared my soul. A trusted family member betrayed my trust. The scars from that experience were not just on my body but on the fabric of my soul. It was the kind of hurt that magnified my detachment, pushing me further into a chasm of despair.

It culminated one cold evening, in an empty neighborhood park. The weight of it all was unbearable, and escape was near. The pills in my hand offered liberation. And then came the internal tug-of-war. A battle between the desire to end it and a faint voice of resilience. I wrestled with the reasons to persist, but darkness prevailed.

Yet, against all odds, the thread of life held, and for a time, in that hospital room, I was suspended in a surreal space between two realms. Amidst the confusion, a glimmer of hope emerged. It was in that room where my new beginning began.

That spark of life within me grew. It was a glimmer that whispered of the latent power within me—a power to shape my narrative, to forge a fresh path. This wasn't the end; it was a crossroads, leading to profound introspection and a newfound purpose.

It was figuratively and physically, the pivotal turning point in my life. Facing the edge of life and death gave me a new perspective on everything. Instead of drowning in sorrow, I felt a strong will to push through.

The promise I made to myself in the hospital wasn't just a passing idea; it was the start of a significant change in my life. I never thought that this dark moment would lead me to discover my true purpose: a journey to inspire and transform others.

The road ahead wasn't easy, but I made a promise to myself: to keep moving forward, to beat the odds, and to never let darkness pull me down again. As days turned into weeks, my pain began to transform into a clear goal. Slowly, I started seeing a life beyond my troubled past, a life worth fighting for.

I discovered a simple truth: The mind, I had learned, was both jailer and liberator. It can keep us stuck, but it can also free us from our darkest moments.

It can wrap us in cycles of doubt and despair, tethering us to the shadows of our past and looming uncertainties. In its restrictive role, it ensnares us in patterns of uncertainty, apprehension, and hopelessness, binding our essence to the burdens of our history and our worries about the days ahead. Such bindings, often born from traumatic events, societal norms, or personal flaws, can create a sense of enduring entrapment, where negativity amplifies our perceived limitations.

Yet, within that mental expanse lies a transformative force of liberation. Recognizing and harnessing this power enables us to rise above challenges, reframing them as pathways to our higher selves. This liberating path pushes us to question our self-imposed limitations and recraft our narrative with hope and purpose. With the right perspective, our minds evolve into our greatest allies, guiding us from darkness toward a future radiant with potential.

When I realized the power of turning hardships into opportunities for growth, my life truly began to change. I started a journey of self-understanding and healing that changed my life's path.

I had never succeeded at school, but now I became determined to overcome all obstacles. Math became my therapy. I graduated with honors to become a math teacher, driven by my passion for helping children who struggled. I worked in many schools before I realized that I did not want to be a part of a broken system, where students were being left behind and teachers were burning out.

So, I quit the classroom to build a business where I work with students privately, one-on-one. There was an undeniable urge compelling me to be a voice for the voiceless and to transform my personal odyssey into a source of hope and motivation for countless others.

This led me to develop what would become a central part of my mission—the Meta-Learning DeStress Method™.

The Meta-Learning DeStress Method™ was created from a mix of my personal struggles, scientific research, and a deep commitment to helping others. Developed and refined over 24 years, this methodology now helps others navigate tough times.

Through time and improvements, the method incorporated aspects of NLP (NeuroLinguistic Programming) and hypnotherapy, aiming to offer a well-rounded strategy for both personal growth and enhanced learning. Too many students who face obstacles in their learning simply do not have the appropriate support or tools to succeed.

My journey to the Meta-Learning DeStress Method™ started from a personal place, but it was enriched because of my own challenges as a student, and my years of experience working as a classroom teacher and a private tutor.

Rooted deeply in the advanced findings of brain research and the intricacies of neurolinguistics, this method unravels the tapestry of human cognition. It serves as a guide, illuminating the often-obscure pathways of our thinking, and offering clear directions for navigating our mind's labyrinthine corridors.

The method acknowledges the inherent challenges that our minds can present. Like vast, uncharted terrains, our brains harbor valleys of doubt and peaks of confidence. But, armed with the right tools, strategies, and insights, these terrains can be transformed into fertile grounds for personal development and evolution.

By gaining a deeper understanding of our cognitive architecture, we empower ourselves to proactively reshape neural pathways, allowing us to reconfigure limiting beliefs and manifest desired behaviors.

It's akin to mastering the art of mental cartography, wherein we chart and re-chart the courses of our minds. It was this profound journey of cognitive mastery, coupled with the drive to share these revelations with others, which paved the way for my metamorphosis into a Learning Success Coach. Through this role, I aspired not only to impart knowledge but also to guide individuals in harnessing their mind's vast potential, turning challenges into opportunities for growth and enlightenment.

As I immersed myself further, it became increasingly evident that my potential to effect change wasn't limited to individual interactions. The transformations I witnessed in my one-on-one coaching sessions made me want to reach more students. I began to envision a ripple effect; a scenario where my teachings and methods wouldn't be constrained by time or personal bandwidth.

This realization sparked the idea of training others in the methodologies and insights I had garnered over the years. By empowering fellow educators with the tools and techniques I had honed, I could amplify my impact manifold.

Not only would this approach facilitate the propagation of my methods to a larger audience, but it would also ensure sustainable reach. Every individual I trained would, in turn, become a beacon of knowledge and guidance for countless students.

This multiplier effect has the potential to reshape the learning landscape, helping numerous students navigate their educational journeys with more confidence and efficacy. Through this expanded vision, I aspired to create a legacy that transcends individual interactions and fosters a community of empowered educators and learners.

Driven by this newfound purpose, I embarked on a mission to equip educators with the Meta-Learning DeStress Method™. Good teachers who are well-equipped are not just transmitters of knowledge, they possess the transformative power to either uplift or hinder a student's growth.

To harness this profound influence, I designed comprehensive training tailored to the unique challenges and dynamics of working with any struggling student.

The training emphasizes the importance of fostering an environment that isn't merely about rote memorization, but one that cultivates resilience, emotional intelligence, and a love for learning.

I have proven that by arming educators with these tools and methodologies, they can inculcate a more adaptive and nurturing learning culture. Through this, students will not only acquire knowledge more effectively but also develop the skills to cope with stress, setbacks, and challenges.

My goal is to light a beacon with each trained educator, as they implement the Meta-Learning DeStress Method™ and in turn create a cascading effect of positive transformations, wherein each student touched by these methods would be better equipped to thrive in both academia and life.

Today, I am proud to say that our company, Success Codes, trains educators from around the world in the Meta-Learning DeStress Method™ and my mission is clear: We aim to reach and assist 1.5 million students by 2035.

I've seen firsthand the incredible transformation that happens when people tap into the untapped potential of their minds. The Meta-Learning DeStress Method™ isn't just about bridging educational gaps; it's about embarking on a continuous journey of self-awareness, resilience, and success.

Here is what some of our Learning Success Coaches are saying:

- "This is a perfect opportunity for those of us who love education and really believe in doing the best thing for kids. It's just so refreshing."

- "It's pretty awesome. It brings the joy back to teaching and helping students learn and grow."

Looking back on the twists and turns that brought me here, I'm overwhelmed with gratitude for the dark moments that ignited my determination. As painful as those times were, they were crucial in helping me discover my true calling and create a positive impact on others.

One clear lesson from this journey is that our purpose isn't something external. It's deeply intertwined with who we are, waiting to be discovered and celebrated. Our purpose embodies our passions, skills, and experiences. It's the unique mark each of us can make on the world, and it's up to us to unveil it.

Ultimately, my journey from struggle to purpose has shown me that the quest to find and live our purpose is deeply transformative. It's about embracing challenges, finding the bright side in difficult times, and using our stories to inspire others. Our purpose goes beyond self; it's about the positive change we bring to the lives of others and the lasting legacy we create.

Looking back on my path, I'm deeply moved by these words:

How will you spend your one wild and precious life?
~Mary Oliver

This sentiment encapsulates my personal mission: to transform hardships into meaningful purposes and make a lasting impact within our short time here.

Embracing one's purpose means not just growing individually, but uplifting the larger community. It's about continuous evolution and embracing change. For instance, the Meta-Learning DeStress Method™ isn't a fixed system but an ever-evolving method designed to aid people in an unpredictable world.

Through my journey, I've recognized that true purpose isn't pursued in isolation. It involves creating connections and partnering with like-minded individuals eager for positive transformation. By creating a community of thinkers, visionaries, and change-makers, we amplify our collective efforts. Together, our combined energy has the power to create waves of change far greater than any of us could achieve alone.

Living one's purpose requires a deep well of resilience—the strength to bounce back from obstacles and confront challenges directly. The journey isn't always a straightforward one; moments of doubt and struggle are bound to arise. However, these moments can be our greatest teachers, strengthening our resilience and inspiring us to refine our strategies to achieve our goals.

The zeal to make a meaningful impact is admirable, but it's equally crucial to ensure we don't neglect ourselves in the process. In our quest to fulfill our purpose, it's essential to prioritize our well-being. Dedicating moments for self-reflection, relaxation, and renewal ensures we have the stamina and clarity to continue our journey with determination.

It's also vital to recognize that purpose isn't a fixed point; it's a dynamic entity that evolves with us. Embracing one's purpose is not a straight path but a cycle of growth, reflection, and action. As we gain more experiences and insights, our sense of purpose grows, leading us to fresh opportunities and deeper satisfaction.

To sum it up, my purpose, carved out of despair and aimed at heights unknown, highlights that finding and embodying one's purpose is an incredibly transformative process. It's about facing adversities, finding beauty in the midst of struggles, and sharing our narratives to uplift others. More than an individual quest, our purpose intertwines with the impact we make on others, leaving a lasting footprint in the sands of time.

So, as we navigate the twists and turns of existence, let's remember that our purpose is not a destination, but a journey of growth, impact, and fulfillment. Let's embrace the challenges and setbacks as steppingstones for growth. Let's foster connections, collaborations, and communities that uplift and support one another. And let's never underestimate the power of our singular, remarkable life to make an enduring difference in the world.

Kohila Sivas

Kohila Sivas is the mastermind behind the groundbreaking MathCodes Method™ and Meta-Learning DeStress Method™. These innovative systems are crafted to help students recover lost learning and make learning more understandable. Built on the foundation of brain science and neurolinguistics, these methods have evolved over 24 years of Kohila's direct work with over 1600+ students who faced learning challenges.

Not stopping there, Kohila has also formulated the Learning Success Coaching training program, tailored for teachers and educators. This endeavor empowers these passionate educators to make a meaningful impact on various types of learners. Learning Success Coaching stands as an all-encompassing coaching approach that proves to be a distinctive and superior alternative to traditional tutoring and teaching methods across all subjects.

With a resolute goal in sight, we aspire to serve 1.5 million students or more by the year 2035. Kohila Sivas is a Coach, Mentor, Marketer, Investor, #1 International Bestselling Author, and a Speaker.

With a visionary mindset, a relentless drive, and the integration of holistic AI marketing, Kohila Sivas continues to redefine education, empower learners worldwide, and leave an indelible mark on the future of learning and on marketing for entrepreneurs.

Connect with Kohila at https://www.learningsuccessacademy.com/.

CHAPTER 13

Tootsie Rolls and Inspiration

Kristin René VanGundy

---

*This book is dedicated to my best friend and soulmate
Lance and our three lovely daughters Hannah, Madisun &
Kelbryn VanGundy. Thank you for giving me purpose with
unconditional love. I am a lucky lady.*

Autumn in the Midwest is my favorite season. The leaves on the trees change their colors from gorgeous greens to vibrant yellows, oranges, and reds. I relish the taste of hot cocoa around a crackling bonfire, being careful not to burn your tongue with the very first sip. After several spoonfuls and taste tests, we artfully craft robust pots of chili and try not to dribble any on our favorite sweaters. Warm cozy blankets come out of storage, and boots tumble out of the closet, all hold memories of the years past.

As a young girl, I remember that fall always had a purpose. For my mother and I, it was more than just the changing of the seasons. It was another opportunity to gather family and friends to our home for a meaningful cause. Every October, my mother would host a fundraising event for the NKF, (National Kidney Foundation). She was a fighter against her own kidney disease and believed that her voice mattered. I would help her set up our small yard, taste-test her amazing chili with all the different kidney beans, and make sure that the hot cocoa was rich and chocolatey.

One of my favorite parts was creating the bags that each volunteer would carry with them. The goodie bags held information on the NKF, and the best part, a secret treasure. Inside were cylinder cans of tootsie rolls and jolly ranchers. Everyone would gather at our small and humble, but very well-decorated trailer home. We would set out in different teams, walking from door to door, asking for any donations in exchange for the candy. This was back in the '70s, well before modern advances in kidney transplant medicine. Our efforts were purposeful in support of medical research.

I don't recall anyone refusing to drop some change or a dollar bill for some yummy candy.

This was one of my very first purposes: to watch and witness my mom being more than just my mom … more than just the disease. I learned many struggles from her, not just as a single parent, but one with the chronic disease of kidney failure. Watching her find her strength with her faith to keep going was powerful. She embodied beauty, while being weak. She demonstrated love and tenderness despite experiencing personal fear and anger. My mom led with a soulful cause, not knowing if any of it would make a difference in time to help her, but believing it would eventually help others.

I know that my mother's sole purpose was to raise me with every ounce of her goodness, despite all her own tragedies and fears.

The year was 1979, and there were plenty of donor kidneys, but not good medications to guard against rejection. After three failed kidney transplants and worn-down veins that could no longer be dialyzed, she passed away. I was only eleven. She was the strongest person that I knew. She was my everything. As an adult, I only now begin to realize the impact her fight left on me. I remember how hard she fought to make this world a better place, always showing up exactly as she was, even through her hardships.

The tootsie rolls may have found their way into my belly as often as a neighbor's hands, but trust me when I say that fall has remained a cherished time of year.

We have many purposes in our lifetime. We can learn not only from our own achievements and failures, but also from those that have paved the way before us.

Many might say finding your purpose is easy because it's finding what truly sets your soul on fire. I used to think that we really had only one purpose. How scary is that? What if it fails? What if it doesn't? What happens when you've completed your purpose? Then what?

Marrying my high school sweetheart was my next big purpose. Choosing to become a life partner was committing to a forever love. I was aware of the decision to choose a love like no other and a soul mate to journey through this life with. This union is still going strong as we celebrate our 34th wedding anniversary. My purpose in this relationship remains true, but also the definitions of this purpose have evolved.

I strive to be constant when everything around us is changing, to be a safe haven when life is uncertain, to be a light when the shadows of darkness creep in, to be the person that laughs and cries with him. I search to allow for splendor to be intentional.

As we have grown as individuals through the years, we have also grown as a couple. We have learned to identify that we each have unique purposes, and yet we share purposes of equal value. All these years later, we understand how to create space for our vulnerability, because in that meaningful choice, our relationship becomes extraordinary. Cultivating this true love has been my heart's chosen purpose.

Raising our three daughters was my next most important purpose. After my mother's example, I never assumed that becoming a mother was going to be easy. I have always asked myself why? Why did I get so lucky to be a mother of three girls? I questioned, how would I do this without the guidance of my own mother? How could I become what they need? There is no manual, after all. Many times, when I was lost with what to do, I would simply ask myself what I would have wanted from my mother in that same situation. The answer would always manifest.

Each of our daughters, in their very own and authentic way, has given me more than I ever knew possible. I didn't always see it then, navigating the stresses of raising children, providing guidance to one daughter about a troublesome boyfriend, while helping another navigate the pressures of mean girls and social media. What I know now: nurtured purpose, with unconditional love, is a mother's soul essence.

Let me tell you, I embraced this purpose. As our youngest daughter was heading off to college, I became highly aware of an intense sadness overcoming me. What was I going to do now? I had poured my heart and soul into these beautiful humans and loved every minute of it. Well … it was the hardest thing I've ever done. I know it was such a gift to bear witness as these gorgeous souls flourished. I knew that it was a good thing that they were finding their own way and experiencing life. But it also meant that I had to finally face myself … after this purpose seemed to be at an end.

What would I fill my time and energy with? I decided to retire from the dance studio where I taught and where our youngest had danced for fifteen years.

I knew that I was seeking something more, but I didn't know what. Hence the question, what would be my next purpose? I loved teaching and supporting girls, instilling self-worth, and confidence, but how could I navigate this passion into my next purpose?

A cherished friend and life coach asked me a defining question. She challenged me with a simple introspection: what do I want? I don't believe that I had ever asked myself this question.

My first answer was to be able to eat all the chocolate that I wanted and for the calories not to count. Silliness aside, I found myself struggling to produce other desires and then affirming them out loud. It was very uncomfortable sitting with myself and yet, coming to the realization that it was okay to discover new things that lit me up. I found joy in giving myself permission to uncover that there was so much more that I wanted to do and experience. I had been serving my heart's purpose for my family, but now it was time to walk over another bridge and see what was on the other side.

Generational conditioning led me to believe that it was selfish to listen and take care of my own needs. Understanding this was a pivotal moment in my life. Choosing myself with these new wants and desires was transformational. I was stepping onto new stones, which allowed me to move forward and show up in my own authentic truth without worrying about everyone else.

This is the golden ticket, the yummy tootsie roll, the chocolatey goodness. Giving ourselves permission to start new chapters and see what is available for us to experience.

So there I was, fresh into my fifties, finding myself while asking some exciting questions. How could I help other women? Could my experiences in life; as a wife, a mother, and a woman who has survived difficult tragedies inspire others? What was my biggest fear? Was I ready to put myself out there and not care what others thought? The thought of stepping out of my comfort zone was terrifying. Who was I now?

My husband was so gracious during this transitional time. He assured me that it was okay to take the time that I needed, to figure out what was next. His exact words, which I still continuously repeat to myself, "It's not a race, but rather a pace in finding what makes me happy."

After several weeks of moping around our very empty house, I scrolled through social media and decided that I needed to read a self-help book. Say what? I was never a big fan of reading, but for some reason, I felt compelled. Oprah has always been my inspirational mentor and goodness guru from afar. I read anything and everything that she has shared.

I began my search and stumbled upon the book, *The Universe Has Your Back* by Gabby Bernstein. Gabby is known as a spirit junkie, an American author, motivational speaker, and podcast host. Her energy was so attractive, and it awakened something within my soul. I was reading and also listening to her audiobooks, while allowing myself to be still.

My new journey began as I started walking over the bridge, seeking answers from myself, for myself. I began a new practice of meditation. I had always been a prayer warrior, but was open to trying something new. I found an application on my cell phone called the *Insight Timer*, which helped me practice connecting with my breath.

It's crazy to think how such a simple thing as releasing random thoughts and focusing on the breath can empower the mind and body.

This practice has given me so much clarity in my search for my next purpose.

I decided to hire a life coach who practiced reiki as well (using life force energy through the body to reduce stress and promote healing.) I had never heard of this before, but was open to trying it. All I can say is that it was transformative. For a year, I dug deep into my childhood trauma. I had long ago tried to ignore the turmoil of losing my mom at such a young age and all the troubled years that followed. Through reiki, I realized that grief had been holding me down, keeping me a prisoner to the sad story of my childhood. I had been carrying this weight for all those years, storing it deep down inside of my body.

Uncovering the truth that I had not fully grieved the loss of my mother, allowed me to understand that I had been in survival mode. After my mother's death, much of my life became a game of pretend. The years after her passing were difficult, and I am still learning how to forgive myself and take full responsibility for the hurt and pain.

I believe that part of my healing process has been letting go of the victim role. Yes, some of my childhood was taken from me, and it was tragic, but I don't believe that my mom did it on purpose. It wasn't her fault that she got sick and passed on. The roles that others played in my guardianship have also left many wounds, but again, I am choosing to release the sad stories, because they are no longer serving me.

Each time that I left a session with my life coach and reiki healer, I became closer to finding me, my most genuine self. These sessions were not easy, but I knew they served a new purpose. I would physically come out of my appointments feeling lighter. I believe that allowing myself to be vulnerable in this state was imperative so that I could heal and move forward, find my new grounding, and what I was being called to do next.

Through the sessions, I came to embrace the notion that I still had more to do, more to discover and experience. I was excited and ready to see what else was possible. I was finding my own truth, not only as a loving wife or a good mom, but in my own soul's essence as Kristin.

I recall one of my reiki sessions when I started receiving beautiful messages. My healer was holding my right hand, and I heard that I was *to write*. Here I am, five years later, still unfolding so much of the goodness that I received. Because I chose to invest in myself and the reiki process, I'm able to sit here and write, using my voice with intention to serve and inspire.

The pressure that we place upon ourselves to have a purpose is undeniable. For many generations, we were conditioned to set and achieve goals and to live by a certain set of standards that had been passed down. When I was a young woman, the patterns modeled for me established several mundane purposes. They were, in order:

First: grow up.

Second: go to school.

Third: get married.

Fourth: have a family.

Fifth: live happily ever after. The end.

That was it. That was the life model many of us grew up with. Where was the understanding that maybe this would work out or maybe it wouldn't? Did I have any other options? Was this supposed to be my only story? I'm lucky that it worked out for me the way it has, but have these been my most authentic divine purposes?

Truly understanding what drives us or gives us meaningful purpose is to ask the important question, what makes us smile from our very soul? This could very well be your chosen career, but as we shift and expand, so might the purpose. If you hear nothing else from my writing, it is this: I want to inspire you to give yourself permission to seek your next purpose.

So now comes the big question, what is it that I'm seeking? After my year of what I like to call an awakening, I discovered that I aspired to inspire. I want to serve women of all ages. I want to give back. I want to start finding my own truths. I want to start taking chances on the uncomfortable and living a life full of enthusiasm and expansion.

This year of transformation helped me see that my journey was only just beginning. I learned that I could be an even better partner to my husband. I find value in holding space for him and in choosing him day after day. We create a collaborative purpose together in authoring the ideal story of our life together.

I've become a student to my grown daughters, allowing them to teach me how to have an open heart and mind about everything. Through them, I have uncovered pieces of myself that I had lost along the way. Their example encouraged me to listen to my own inner knowing for who I wanted to become: a vessel to help other women heal and find their own inner essence, radiating a light to guide with grace, goodness, and love.

As you read these chapters from all these amazing women, I know that you are seeking more. You wouldn't have chosen this book if you weren't.

So how do I find my purpose?

How do you find your purpose?

Take time to sit with yourself and ponder the following questions. More, give yourself permission to invest in yourself and seek out new possibilities.

What gets me excited to get out of bed in the morning?

Where do I spend a lot of my time, energy, and money? Is that where I want to invest myself?

What comes with ease while also challenging me? Where do I find joy and fulfillment?

Am I sharing my gifts and talents to help others? How can I pay it forward with intentionality.

Surrounding yourself with positive and like-minded people will also help you to rise to what else might be calling you. Who are you spending most of your time with? Do they inspire you to be the very best version of yourself? Do you feel uplifted or emotionally drained? Could it be time to say no to something that is no longer filling up your cup? Choose to release it so that you can make room for something different.

Sometimes, we must step out of our comfort zone and try something new. Believe it or not, we get to create most of our experiences. What we allow into our minds and spaces directly affects us. For example, if I turn on the TV first thing in the morning, I'm starting my day with outside sources that will most likely flavor my experience, often with negativity. Alternately, if I choose to listen to meditative music first, then I get to set my intentions for how I want the day to flow. I give myself the power to control my mindset and the start of my day.

Our choices regarding what we internalize from the outside reflect into us, into our very core. We get to choose where our energy comes from as well as who gets to receive it.

One last thought, not everyone has to find a new purpose. Your life might be exactly the way it is supposed to be at this given time. There is still tremendous value in allowing yourself to slow down and step back from all the things that just keep you busy. Because sometimes, all the trappings of life are just that, keeping busy. Find time to be with yourself and reflect on where you have been and where you might want to go. You might find that you're content and feel fulfilled with your life and only need to acknowledge the people, places, and experiences that have seasoned you and given you purpose. Or you might find there is an opportunity to allow a new purpose to flourish. As for me, I'm going to unwrap a tootsie roll and consider my options.

Kristin VanGundy

Kristin VanGundy is an Essence Coach, speaker, believer in the power of light & love and Reiki energizer. She believes in the power of still allowing every day to be a gift by living in the present and on purpose!

She is passionate about helping women of all ages find their voice and power from within. Her mission as an Essence Coach is to help women uncover their authentic self and heal their mind-body-soul connection so they can reclaim their power, find true purpose, and live a life filled with joy, peace, and love.

She uses her intuition, spirituality, and energy-healing abilities to guide clients toward a better understanding of themselves and their true calling in this world. She also works with them on creating a lifestyle to reach their full potential—a life that's in harmony with the mind, body, and soul.

Kristin draws on lessons learned in forging a successful marriage and has been married to her high school sweetheart of almost 35 years. She is a mother of three amazing grown daughters and a proud Pawrent of two sheepadoodles! Kristin and her husband reside at a lake home in Unionville Mo.

Some of her other passions are thoughtful interior design, music, immersion in nature activities, leisure time with family and of course, all things chocolate.

Connect with Kristin at https://www.kristinvangundy.com.

CHAPTER 14

Living on Purpose

Laura Diaz

I dedicate this chapter to all those people who have been in my life and have helped me find my purpose.

Live the life you have been postponing.
Increase your courage and speak your truth.
Use courage to take you places you have been wanting to go,
Places you have been dreaming.
Courage will ignite your voice,
Your bold expression of who you are,
And then,
You will come alive.

Live on purpose and start claiming you.
Live on purpose with intention.
Life is now,
Not tomorrow

In the later part of 2010, as I was approaching my 60th birthday, I felt a subtle restlessness inside asking me to make a change in my work.

There I was with 30 plus years at a good job as a civil service employee, with great benefits and working environment. But at the same time, something inside of me was whispering that it was time for a change.

A transformation was coming. My intuitive feelings were telling me the change could not be completed at that place of employment, as a team manager!

"What is that about?"

I remember as a child, I would frequently ask myself deep questions such as:

"Why am I here?"

"What do I want to do when I grow up?"

"What is my purpose in life?"

Beginning at the age of four-years-old and continuing through different phases of my life, these were questions I frequently asked.

As time moves on, we are constantly wanting to find out why we are here in this world. The interesting thing is that our life purpose emerges as we grow and experience more in our lives.

The questions that we ask are answered during our development into adulthood, as we gain more wisdom and experience.

Maybe that is how we find our purpose in life.

Getting Started in Finding My Purpose

I liked my job as a manager, and at the same time, I wanted to explore the next chapter of my life. I did not feel that I was engaging to my full potential as a Team Manager. There was a void that was calling to me and wanted expression.

Maybe, my purpose was looking for me and this was the time for me to make that move.

What was next for me? This quest for answers led me to hire a life coach, to help me explore these intuitive nudges. I needed guidance that was consistent with my longing to leave my present employment.

During my life coaching experience, I became fascinated with the coaching I was receiving. Not only did this process clarify my personal thoughts, but it also suggested the answer for the next phase of my life!

I was very curious about what was next for me. Was this a time of reinvention?

As I reflect back on this moment, I know I was being guided by my intuitive feelings and whispers. This was a big decision, and I remember learning during college that there was a method to use in making a decision. It was certainly not using intuitive guidance and nudges!

I worked with my life coach for about five months and decided that I, too, wanted to train in life coaching. Becoming a life coach was a natural transition on my journey into retirement. The decision to be trained as a life coach felt right. It was a new adventure that was calling a part of me to engage and reveal my true expression.

I was so proud of myself for having the courage and intention to start a new career!

The Thread of Becoming

I believe this thread of finding my purpose and becoming a life coach began for me in the 1990s.

It started when I decided to find my voice ...

Have you ever been in a situation in which you had to make a difficult choice? A choice between a better future or a safe present? A choice to either face a BIG FEAR or compromise on your goals? If so, then you know it's not easy.

One day, I had made the choice that I wanted upward mobility and didn't want to be passed over for promotion. I was ready to empower myself and deal with my fear of speaking in front of people. This fear was holding me back from being promoted and from asking for help.

I wanted to succeed in my career and I wanted more administrative/ managerial positions. When I realized it was important that I speak confidently in front of groups, I did my research and joined a speaking group, called Toastmistress, that would train me how to speak in public.

For a long time, I had believed I couldn't speak in front of people. During high school and college, I didn't have the confidence or courage to speak in class. I had been hesitating for the first 30 years of my life to speak in front of groups! I remember the embarrassing and tense moments I experienced when the teacher would call on me during class and I was asked to stand and speak. I would feel afraid and nervous as I started to speak.

One of my core beliefs is that we all have a message and if you find a way to speak and share your gifts and talents, you'll make a significant contribution to others, as well as, to yourself.

Now, I can speak with ease and confidence in front of groups. I enjoy being a teacher, speaker and life coach and leading classes and groups. I feel good about who I am and what I'm expressing through my words. My beliefs have changed significantly through the choice I made of asking for help with training and practice in being a professional speaker and teacher. My activities now include speaking often with small groups and classes.

I believe that for me to live my purpose, I had to overcome the fear of public speaking. Overcoming this fear opened opportunities and it opened me to myself!

My self-confidence was lifted due to overcoming a big fear and accomplishing a big goal!

Realizing that you have a choice to make every day is a realization to make a choice that will advance you in being your authentic self.

Choosing to create a better version of myself every day is a choice. My choice to engage in learning public speaking was an empowering choice for me, because it opened many doors that have led me to finding my purpose.

Having self-confidence was important, because it meant I would ignite my courage in being open to trying new things. It meant freedom!

As I reviewed my journals from 2014, I noticed that as I journaled, a new emerging awareness was taking place. During that time, I was engaged in studying spirituality with my church, Center for Spiritual Living. I was also taking personal development courses that helped accelerate my professional skills as a coach.

I noticed an optimistic attitude as I woke up in the mornings. I was expecting a day filled with good, peace and harmony. The good thing about this focus was that the more I saw good around me, the more I experienced abundance in my life!

This new-ness insight was coming through me as a spiritual wake-up and it felt like a *new Light* that was being turned on.

I embraced a new level of listening, centering, and allowing for the flow of new ideas to come forth.

Journaling has been a meditative practice for me. I used my writing to focus, decide, and plan.

I had just retired from a long work history of 34 years in late 2012. As a new entrepreneur, I was building a coaching business without much training on how to create a business. So, I started small by taking some business development classes and hiring a mentor coach.

I realized during my spiritual development that it was best for me to feel strong about my choice to become a life coach. So, I decided to invest my time with my faith and learning spiritual principles. My studies supported my choice of becoming the best life coach I could be.

The increased awareness of my spirituality was essential in realizing that I was living on purpose with the work I was doing as a life coach. During this unfolding of myself, I was birthing a new confidence of who I was becoming and being!

I Decided to Become a Life Coach

Towards the end of being coached in 2011, I explored several coaching programs and choose a program in San Diego, Accomplishment Coach Training program, which was in person for one year.

I decided to attend one of their observation Saturdays, where new prospects can observe the current class being trained. When I observed the live class of coaching students being trained for Life Coaching, I knew this was the place for me!

As I listened to the facilitator teach the new coaching students, I experienced a strong intuitive feeling come over me that whispered, "*You are home*! *This is it!*"

At that moment, I felt like a light was turned on inside of me!

The new me was emerging with strength and faith in becoming a life coach!

I learned that listening to your inner voice and acting with courage strengthens the new you that is exploring change in your life.

Somehow everything seemed to be coming together with a synchronicity that I cannot explain.

As I experienced this emotional embrace, I decided that this (life coaching) was my next career!

How will I make this happen? I did not have the answer, but I trusted that I would find the resources. I did find financial resources that helped me fund my one-year coaching training program.

My choice to train in life coaching and leave my corporate job has given me many happy, meaningful, joyous moments!

As a life coach, I have experienced more joy, freedom, courage, love, and creativity. I feel I have stretched my potential and creativity. My choice to move into the life coaching professional was the start of me reinventing who I was as a person and as a professional. This choice helped me realize how to live my purpose, because I came alive with the new learning, beingness, and expression of myself, with ease and flow as a life coach and a teacher.

I feel a sureness in what I am doing. I enjoy helping others find their purpose in life.

Purpose is spirit seeking expression; awareness of it allows
us to see our lives more clearly from the inside out.
~Kevin Cashman, Leadership from the Inside Out

During my early years as a life coach, I defined my life purpose:

My purpose is to be of service to the Infinite Universe and
be an expression of Good, so I can inspire others toward
Goodness, Harmony, Joy, and live a life of their dreams.
~Laura Diaz

Reflection That I Am on Purpose

One morning, as I was facilitating a personal enrichment class at San Diego Oasis, I noticed something different. The class was going well and the audience was responding in a very positive manner. They asked questions and made comments about the topic and materials I was presenting.

What was amazing and very surreal was, as I was talking to the class, it was as if someone else was also talking through me and expressing my deep wisdom. After this first time, I noticed that these uncanny moments would happen occasionally during different classes!

As I completed each class, I would pause and reflect on the moments of spiritual wisdom that had come through. I gave thanks to the Universe in supporting me through each class and sharing its wisdom.

During my first few years as a life coach, I was consistently growing and re-defining my work. I believed then and still believe that this inner wisdom was *Infinite Wisdom* speaking through me. I was supported by this Higher Wisdom, and I knew I was living my life on purpose.

I re-discovered my passions that motivated me, which are reading, learning, working with small groups and problem-solving. My intention was to help others find a positive outlook about themselves and the world.

I claimed my work as my purpose when I named my coaching business, In Harmony Coaching. I claimed my spot in this field by creating a website and announcing that I was open for business.

My mission has been to educate, guide and coach women towards building their self-confidence and independence.

I was very clear that the work I was doing as a life coach, speaker, and teacher was in alignment with my life purpose ... AND I was here to be of service to BECOMING a bigger version of myself, as I helped others become a bigger version of themselves.

Finding my purpose has been a path to finding my calling. When I realized that offering my services as a life coach was a platform for expression of my creativity, talents, and values, I re-affirmed that I was in the right place. I also found a new lasting happiness.

Living with intention and purpose is a life of living with happiness and joy!

Laura Diaz

Laura Diaz is a professional trained life coach. She is the founder of In Harmony Coaching, a company whose mission is to inspire and increase women's confidence so that they are empowered to create a life they love.

Laura specializes in helping women create compelling goals, accelerate their results, and create richer, more fulfilling lives. For over 30 years, Laura, has been studying and implementing transformational success principles, and as a sought-after speaker, trainer and certified coach, Laura's workshops and coaching programs help people breakthrough limitations, limiting beliefs and supports her clients achieve greater results.

Her coaching has helped women discover their potential and live from a place of confidence, passion, and freedom, while building their wealth and creativity. She is passionate about helping women move through difficult times and provide them the tools and training so they can transition from uncertainty to confidence.

She is a Board-Certified Coach (BCC) and received her board certification in June 2018.

She self-published her first book on Amazon: Choose Confidence: 21 Ways Women Can Increase Self-Confidence. She is an international best-selling author for the collaboration book, Action Takers Who Get Shit Done.

Connect with Laura at https://www.inharmonycoaching.com.

CHAPTER 15

Walk With Me

Niki Hall

I don't think you determine what your purpose is.
I think you discover what your purpose is.
~Bob Proctor

I've heard it said so many times by some very strong and bigger-than-life personalities, "Your purpose is your reason for living." Humm! That statement, said in that manner, makes me feel like I don't have a purpose for living. Then my thoughts quietly inside myself, and pathetically, would say to myself, "Oh that's bad." Hey! Wait a minute! We can't all be Mother Theresa. We should be realistic about where the height of that bar is when it comes to thinking about our personal purposes. Often our thoughts are way out in the cosmos and, of course, we can't relate. But the truth is many of us, perhaps in more than any other time period, are growing and moving toward a better life. Thus, living on purpose.

We know it isn't easy, but we also know living on purpose will bring us a sense of fulfillment that is true to ourselves and is something we can only achieve intellectually. We know it's about bringing our genuine gifts to the surface and using them to provide good service and to take our natural place in the game of life.

Perhaps it would be better if I heard the questions, "Who is moving toward living on purpose?" and "Where are you at with it?" Hearing it stated in this way, my subconscious accepts this as the fact that I am working on it and the question is, where am I at with it? It doesn't bring me into that feeling of lacking accomplishment place. And it doesn't make me feel bad or less than, either. It would, the subconscious that is, simply search itself and state exactly where it is in regard to my living on purpose and where it will continue going with sincere intentions while reflecting upon a well-thought-out growth pattern. Now, that feels better.

During COVID-19, a lot of people had time to sit back and take a good look at their lives, their choices, their work, why they made those choices, and why they stuck it out for so long, too long. They found themselves asking "Why? Why? Why?" The result was a record number of people who left their employment. This is a definite reflection of the question … "Are we living on purpose?" A large number of people, upon quiet reflection, answered a resounding, "No," for various reasons. The COVID-19 pandemic time period, sometimes mentioned as *The Great Resignation* has created some big changes. In the U.S., there is a staggering percentage of people who made a career change; 47 million people left their jobs in the year 2021, and roughly, another, 38 million left their jobs in the year 2022. There is a big statement here about living on purpose and moving forward to achieve your personal goals and fulfill your sense of purpose.

Here's some interesting information for those who were already on the obvious road to change just prior to COVID-19. Let's assume they started their personal journey trek in the years 2019 and 2020. Plus, a small portion of these people was right at the beginning of The Great Resignation time period. On September 21, 2022, Credit Suisse's annual report stated that in the year 2021, five point two million people became millionaires. Two and a half million of these millionaires were from the U.S. In the year 2022, there is talk of record millionaires again. The stats vary, but it isn't uncommon to see a statement like, "There is an incredible rise of millionaires again in the year 2022. Roughly eight-point eight percent of the adult population in the U.S. are now millionaires." So, I dare to say, "Many of us are working on it. Living our purpose that is." Even though it seems challenging to attain, many of us are willing to step into that discomfort zone and move to where we think we should be.

There is a wide breadth and a deep depth to living on purpose. I, like my darling Grans, have my own perspectives on that question. Walk with me while I take you on this very personal journey. I say very personal because each and every one of us has our own unique story about how we are growing in our personal purpose in life. This is mine.

A few decades ago, my Grans lived past her 100th birthday. A few years after her landmark birthday, while she was reconciling with the fact that everything was slowing down and beginning to fail her, she had the nurse call me into the hospital before visiting hours. The nurse said my Grans was quite excited about something and she insisted she couldn't wait until visiting hours to share it with me. The nurse gladly called, and minutes later, I was on my way.

The room had a different feeling to it than it usually had. Grans had a youthfulness and wit about her that I hadn't seen in some time. I leaned forward, gently kissed her cheek, and said hello. She smiled and looked brightly at me and said, "I learned my last lesson today." I leaned forward, preparing myself for what I was about to hear. She told me she would not be sharing this time. I assured her she didn't have to share. We were both comfortable with that.

A few peaceful moments later, she was looking pensive. I sat down, braced myself, and took both her hands into mine. As I was trying to prepare myself for a possible difficult conversation, Grans said, "I'm leaving today." I looked at her and I could clearly see she meant what she said and believed every word. She knew she was leaving today. She was so very content and pleased. We celebrated that. She passed a few hours after this conversation.

Grans and I had a great bond together because we both lived our lives on purpose. We both were on a path with a specific end goal in mind. She told me that day that she had learned her last lesson and she had completed her end goal. She felt her gift for doing so well was her leaving this earth to serve and live in a new form which she strongly felt she earned. She felt she earned herself a great place in the vast cosmos that was reflective of all her goodwill, charity, conviction, and hard work. Also, her discipline to stay on course, no matter what tried to stand in her way, challenge her, or downright stop her. Of course, to accomplish this, she had to continuously become the best version of herself that she knew she could be.

I was privileged to witness this fabulous lady at the end of her course of life action, knowing she's done well and has achieved her final goal. As we all know after getting started on our own life's intentional path, it's a personal sense of purpose that is an ongoing impactful pathway that eventually has an end goal to it. It's the whole life game. It's all your dimensions and the accomplishments that are of you. It's you, becoming the best person you can be, by serving, giving of your gifts, and constantly growing and changing until there is no more of you to develop. Which seems impossible, but if we are to follow the example of dear Grans. It can be done.

She made it all look like it was worth it. Every little bit of it. The good, the bad, the challenges, the constant discipline of knowing your direction and sticking to it, and their rewards. That whole big picture revealed itself in one sweet, frail, tiny woman with the heart of a lion. This moved me beyond words. With seeing, relating, and understanding this kind of conviction, Grans made it easy for me to not fear the unknown. To not fear the challenges one faces when you know your mind and happen to be going in a direction that is different from most around you. If not everyone around you.

I was fortunate enough to have two strong-minded women in my life, Grans, of course. However, we never really connected until I was in my early twenties and my Aunt Gena. She was my guiding light all of my childhood, teen years, and adult life. Through my 20s and 30s, during a formidable time of my sculpting out the form of the me I knew I could become, I had two women who knew exactly what they were about, where they were going, and what their purpose was. While I was still laying the foundation for my world, I had these two wonderful women who stood on either side of me. When a heavy wind blew and was about to send me for a tumble, these two women stood strong on each side of me to make sure I wouldn't stumble or fall.

These two women knew who they were, knew where they were going, and knew that nothing was going to stop them from achieving their personal goals and life purpose. Although we were, all three of us, from different decades, we were all the same when it came to ageless vision, determination, and grit. I truly don't know how it is or was for other people, but I can tell you from watching these two ladies and speaking from my own experience, that some of these growth periods or stages one has to move past to stay on purpose are downright hard. It felt hurtful and well, let's say it was challenging. It's also worth it. I don't think I could stress any of these points enough.

Unlike the other two ladies in this interesting combination of people, I knew my ultimate end purpose when I was four years old. I say ultimate because as I grew and accomplished my goals that serve my purpose changed. Most times those goals were part of my purpose. I'm referring to becoming my own person, being a spouse, being a mother, and being a career woman. All of these were, at one point, my sole purpose. They now are a part of who I am to achieve my ultimate goal.

It's very interesting taking this journey when you really don't know what is going on. Really! I had no idea. I simply became aware and briefly experienced the *finger of God*. No kidding! In that moment I was awe-struck and was almost completely able to utter the most important sentence of my life. That was, "Wow! I want to be," and in a microsecond, everything went back to real life, and I had to finish the sentence on my own. The entire statement I was looking to say was "Wow! I want to be with you." Or something to that effect. I was four.

In that precious spiritual experience, things within me, in my little understanding, were re-arranged. There were times when I simply knew right from wrong or that I should or couldn't do certain things if I wanted to keep my eyes on God. While some things became re-arranged for me that allowed me to discern better. I knew enough to listen to that little voice within me saying, "Yeah! Don't do that."

I knew I was a little different than the other kids because their differences would make me cry and feel things I didn't care for. Also, I had a little wisdom to know better not to tell anyone that Jesus was the imaginary friend I was talking to, giving a shoulder ride to, and having my little tea parties with. I didn't want people laughing at me mocking me in some way or telling me I couldn't have Jesus Christ as my imaginary friend. I kept Him my secret. I still feel He is my dear friend, confidant, and trusted guiding light even today.

Let's go back again to my childhood. I had figured out that I wanted to be married and be a parent, as well as have a career of some sort to provide me with the character and vehicle I would need to become the person I was striving to become. I knew my image of myself was a bigger more diversified character than I was.

When I was in the sixth grade, my teacher saw me struggling because I wanted to be like these images of some of the ladies I saw on TV. They were sophisticated and they knew how to do things a certain way. My teacher actually recognized what I was trying to do and now she too knew, I had no idea what I was doing and she discretely, one day, gave me a book that said *Manners Made Easy*. I had no idea I could actually learn this by reading. What a revelation! An entirely new world became possible for me.

Living as a child and now moving into my teens, brought all sorts of new challenges to stay on point or purpose. I didn't have any kind of profound wisdom but, every once in a while, I would hear my own quiet voice say, "Don't do that or don't go there." I could actually feel a sense of going off the beaten track, my keeping my eyes on God and wanting to go His way would be out of my view screen. With that, I had a lessened sense of my spiritual attachment. I didn't want to do that so I had to endure a lot of strange behaviors from those who couldn't figure out why I wouldn't do certain things or tell them why. That was a built-in feeling or sense that I followed. It was years, if not a decade, later when I first heard one of my mentors say, "Don't tell people your goals, keep them private." I know we all have innate wisdom. That simply was one of mine. It saved me from so much misery, several times. I probably can't even count the number.

In high school, I knew the type of man I was going to marry, and again, I didn't fit that mold or socioeconomic standing. I knew I had to take another quantum jump forward. I needed faith and to go! Go! Go! I did and I married into a different lifestyle than I was accustomed to and I was with the man of my dreams.

Many growths and changes happened over the years. The result is I love my life, the people in it, where I live, the work that I do, and the life that I lead.

Because I was so young and because I made a spiritual dedication at that time, a lot of assumptions existed. Like living your purpose. When I started doing research on living on purpose, I came across all these suggestions and steps. I'm reading them and hearing myself say, "Yes." I was consistently in agreement with all these well-thought-out points of understanding and action. I kept looking and looking, yet I couldn't find it. I couldn't find where it tells me to always and continuously cultivate or grow my spiritual connection. That innate ability to intuitively understand meaning and depths of things that further your purpose and ultimately move you forward, to who YOU are. In your foundation for growth, you need that quiet intuitiveness that impacts your soul and validates your meaning and purpose.

Your spiritual connection validates your meaning, it causes a wellness in you that brings deeper inner meaning and growth in life. it allows you to feel a connection, a harmony with your higher power and those around you. It's almost like you constantly take the shortcut home. In my opinion, this is an essential and integral piece of the plan to successfully live on purpose.

These are some of the things my spiritual connection has done for me. It naturally took on my character and moved me into this highly functional way of living:

- Sending an angel to me in the sixth grade opened my eyes to the power of reading. Reading is one of the best ways to broaden your understanding and expand on wisdom. I have never stopped reading, since it was introduced to me so that I could learn about myself.

- Through my Grans, I felt affirmed that living in a growth mindset is the best way to live. I agree. Really, I couldn't have a growth mindset without a purpose. My growth mindset has shown me that I can handle challenges better, and even see them as opportunities at times. It helps me to persevere instead of feeling inferior, inadequate, or incapable. It gives me confidence.

- It opened my eyes to the purpose of being part of a community. Being part of a community gave me personal affirmation, while my assistance was of value to others. I love living in a sense of community.

- Through simply living in the presence of mind that I so very briefly had a taste for, I found myself living more and more in a state of gratitude. It's a lifestyle for me that brings a strengthened sense of purpose, it stimulates a response in my brain that allows me to feel a sense of personal validation. I love living in a state of gratitude. This really works and naturally moves my life forward in ways I couldn't have imagined.

This is how I choose to live my life. I will continue to attain goals and achieve more purposes. I have yet to accumulate enough to become the person I was ultimately created to be. My journey is vast and fun, full of challenges, joys, and surprises. There is no better way that I could have chosen to live my life. I hope to eventually realize that wonderful sense of purpose and completion, as Grans did. In the meantime, there is more growth and fun to be had.

Niki Hall

Niki Hall is a Mindset Coach. Realizing her personal ability to help people, she opened a self-help school. She later wrote a book entitled, Building Up - Thoughts Expressed During the Readjustment of Self. A book on Change and Self-Actualization, where her first printing sold out within days of its release. This catapulted her into public speaking and workshop engagements.

Earlier this year, Niki published two #1 bestselling author stories that shed light on manners of growth and your ability to further establish attitudes for personal gain.

Now Niki has hung a shingle out to help people break through their limited beliefs and to achieve more prosperity in their health, wealth, or business, through the better understanding and application of mindset.

Connect with Niki at https://www.facebook.com/niki.hall.148.

CHAPTER 16

Finding Your Voice

Renee Reisch

This chapter is dedicated to my mom, the woman who gave me life, and showed me love. To my best friend watching over me from heaven who taught me to never give up and to believe in myself. To my dad, also watching over me, who always said "keep the faith, baby." I will dad. And to you, the reader, looking to break free from your own chains; may the words you read resonate along the journey of finding your voice.

In the quest to discover one's purpose, a critical milestone often emerges. One where we finally uncover our unique voices—the authentic expressions of who we are and for what we stand. Just as a compass will point the way through uncharted territories, finding your voice guides you toward aligning with your purpose. In this chapter, I delve into my personal journey of finding my voice and how it propelled me toward the mission of finding my purpose.

Coming from over 25 years in corporate America, I always did more than what was expected of me ... a lot more! So much so that I confused being seen, heard, and valued for who I was, with what I achieved. The more successful I was with my given tasks, the more tasks I was given to accomplish. It became a vicious cycle of wanting to please people at my own expense. I put self-care on the back burner. My best friend was able to clearly observe what I was doing to myself and tried numerous times to stop me from this destructive behavior ... but I never listened. I would always tell her, "I had to do this, and I had to do that." I planned my days off to do more work, rather than take time to recuperate from the long days and nights I had just labored.

It wasn't until I became sick and had to take a Leave of Absence from work that I was forced to stop the cycle. It started with a trip to Urgent Care with one very large and painful sore in the center of my throat. The following day, I woke up in even more pain and called my best friend who drove me back to Urgent Care. The doctor took one look at my throat and told her to get me to the Emergency Room immediately! That one sore had broken out into a multitude of sores covering my vocal cords, leaving me in severe pain, and taking away the one instrument I was privileged to play ... my voice. While in the ER, I recall asking the doctor if I was contagious. He told me I was so contagious that I was no longer allowed to be with the public! Those words hit me like a sucker punch in the gut! That included being with my best friend, my family ... everyone! I sat in my own muck for close to four months. When doctors were unable to find a cure for me, and I didn't know how to find relief for myself, I felt a sense of helplessness and hopelessness and spiraled into a deep depression. My voice, which

I had taken for granted, was now a distant memory. Life, as I had once known it, had changed. It would be a long journey back to restored health and I didn't know if I would ever be able to return to it. It took close to a year, along with the help of an incredible vocal coach, for me to fully regain the use of my voice. *That* was just a small part of it, the external voice. It was the *internal* voice, the inner dialogue, which needed the most healing. Unbeknownst to me, this would turn out to be a pivotal time in my life. It took losing my voice to begin the journey of finding my voice and finding my purpose.

Unveiling Authenticity

For many years I had allowed the noise of external influences to overpower my own desires. Unveiling our unique voice requires us to be vulnerable and honest with ourselves. Authenticity is the cornerstone of finding our purpose and expressing it through our voice. It's about embracing our quirks and flaws, as well as acknowledging our strengths and having the courage to present our true selves to the world. As I embarked upon my journey, I learned that my true voice wasn't about conforming to society, it was about embracing my individuality and expressing my thoughts and feelings in a genuine way.

Finding my voice has not been a linear process, but an exploration into the core of my being, a path that was riddled with self-doubt. I confronted a litany of emotions including anger, grief, confusion, and fear of rejection and judgment. My journey in life has been an ongoing work in progress, one where I slowly shed layers along the way. Doing the inner work is never easy; however, I realized that the more we ignore things we are meant to face, the more they keep showing up. Face your fears, difficult as they may seem, but don't do it alone. I didn't know this would be the path I would end up on after working in corporate America for so many decades, but it *is* the path I now know I needed to be on to fulfill my purpose.

This journey reminds me of *The Wizard of Oz*. Each character had within them the very thing they were seeking outside of themselves. The Scarecrow was looking for a brain, the Tinman was looking for a heart, the Cowardly Lion was looking for courage and Dorothy was looking to find her way back home. When we are out of alignment with who we are, the path to finding our voice and our purpose becomes blurred. Getting back into alignment takes one thing … courage. Although *The Wizard of Oz* was a fictional story, it holds much truth. The "Cowardly" Lion, who was looking for courage, exhibited a tremendous amount when it came to protecting his friends against the Wicked Witch of the West. Similar to the character, when we get out of our heads, we are able to manage obstacles that come up and reframe them into opportunities. The *Yellow Brick Road* that leads us back home to our authentic selves has been there the whole time … it comes from within.

The Uncharted Territory of Emotions

Emotions are complex, intricate threads woven into our lives. They have the power to shape our thoughts, influence our decisions, and even mold our perception of the world. Despite their impact, many of us struggle to navigate this emotional landscape effectively.

My own journey towards understanding emotions began with acknowledging the discomfort they brought. As a society, we are often conditioned to suppress or deny certain emotions that are thought of as negative such as anger, fear, or even sadness; however, these emotions hold immense wisdom if we take a moment to listen.

It was during a period of introspection that I realized emotions aren't enemies needing to be conquered, but rather allies to be understood.

They are clues to the thoughts and beliefs I had been holding onto for decades. They point toward unresolved wounds, unhealed traumas and limiting beliefs that need our attention. This gave me the understanding that my emotions are a connection between my emotional responses and my past experiences.

Unmasking Triggers: A Road to Self-Discovery

Triggers, those emotional landmines that set off intense reactions within us, can be powerful signposts on our journey of self-discovery. Learning to recognize and navigate triggers is an essential skill in finding your voice and aligning with your purpose. I invite you to take a moment and reflect upon how you can use your emotions to serve you in this way too.

For me, identifying triggers was like deciphering a code that had been influencing my actions for years. Through deep introspection and seeking support from peers and mentors, I uncovered patterns that stemmed from earlier experiences, as well as societal conditioning. I am a work in progress, as many of us are. It is a choice. When I notice I have allowed a trigger to control my reaction, I now use it as a tool to reflect upon and create a better way to respond.

Triggers, when approached with curiosity and compassion, become valuable tools for understanding ourselves better. They offer us the opportunity to rewrite old narratives and choose new responses aligned with our ever-evolving sense of purpose.

While it's crucial to acknowledge and explore our emotions, it's equally important not to become entangled with them. Our emotions are part of us, but they do not define us. The ability to detach from them allows us to gain a broader perspective and make decisions from a place of clarity rather than reactivity. Detachment doesn't imply suppression or denial, rather it's a practice of holding them gently and becoming the observer without being consumed, thus allowing them to lose their grip on us.

Harnessing Emotions for Personal Growth

Every emotion we experience holds a lesson, an opportunity for growth and transformation. Anger can illuminate boundaries that need strengthening; fear can reveal areas where we're holding back; sadness can help us process loss and change. By embracing our emotions, we tap into a wealth of self-knowledge that can guide us toward our purpose.

The journey of finding my voice was marked by moments of intense emotional exploration. I learned that rather than suppressing or escaping my emotions, I could channel them into creative outlets like writing, physical activities and speaking. These outlets have become bridges between my inner world and my external expression. They infuse our endeavors with authenticity and depth, creating connections that resonate with others on a profound level.

Lessons Along the Way

Along my journey, there were valuable lessons hidden in the corners of my experiences. It's interesting how setbacks, those things we often try to sweep under the rug, or suppress within ourselves, become setups for growth. Each stumbling block becomes a steppingstone, each misstep, an opportunity to evolve.

I learned that my voice is not confined to success stories alone; it resonates in moments of failure. I have been able to weave resilience, learning and determination from my struggles and turn them into strengths. Sharing these stories has become a cathartic process I didn't know I needed. It helped me connect with others who had encountered similar experiences. Associating with those who have gone through or are going through comparable struggles connects us at a deeper level. While it's undeniably uplifting to hear about people's triumphs and successes, there's a unique power in being able to connect through the challenges they face. It's within these trials, these moments of adversity, that truly bind us in ways that success stories alone might not achieve. Our individual experiences tint the lens through which we view our paths, but when we open up and share our stories with others, we become more relatable.

By revealing our own vulnerabilities and recounting our struggles, we step off the pedestal of flawless accomplishment and become approachable and human. It's a reminder that our journey is comprised of highs and lows, not just an uninterrupted climb to the top. In showing others our less polished parts, we provide them with reassurance that the challenges they face are part of the bigger picture, and more importantly that they are not alone. In my work with others, I have witnessed transformative paths unfold, where individuals step out of the shadows of their own doubts and fears and into the light of their authentic selves.

The power of vulnerability lies in the ability to bridge the gap between our own struggles and those of others. It's a bridge constructed not of bricks and mortar, but of shared experiences and emotions. When we expose our own sensitivity, we openly acknowledge our moments of doubt and difficulty. It is in these moments that we are also extending an invitation for others to join us in a space where authenticity reigns supreme. There is no judgment or justification, only love.

In the realm of personal growth and self-discovery, it's easy to feel isolated, as if your challenges are unique and insurmountable. However, when someone we admire or respect shares their own struggles, it's like a beacon of light breaking through the darkness. It is a powerful reminder that no one is immune to challenges and that the road to self-discovery is a path with many nuances, filled with both triumphs and tribulations.

Every time we embrace our vulnerability, we become more approachable, shedding the protective armor that may have once served us, but because we are no longer that person, it no longer does. It's a brave act, one that requires courage and a willingness to set aside expectations of perfection. And yet, it's this very act that resonates with others, inviting them to do the same.

The Liberation of Expression

Imagine how liberating it would be to realize you're not alone, that your mess ups weren't so unique, and that someone else had faced similar storms and still rose above them to find their voice. These stories unite us with empathy and understanding where we cheer each other on, hold each other up, and celebrate the journey with all the bumps and bruises we collected along the way.

I discovered that my voice held the power to transform moments of self-doubt into threads of connection. Through the power of my words, I extended a hand to those who were navigating through rough waters, offering them the reassurance they needed to emerge stronger. Sharing my experiences has become an act of service.

The beauty of this process is in the reciprocity. As I continued to share, I not only offered solace, but also found continued healing for myself. By putting my experiences into words and sharing them, I was also putting together pieces of my own narrative. It has been a testament to the transformative power of sharing our voices.

As I align with my purpose, a profound and unexpected ripple effect begins to take shape. What was once a solitary journey from my own self-discovery, has now transformed into something far greater. The threads of my story, woven with authenticity and vulnerability, cast a wide net, touching the lives of others in ways I couldn't have imagined. It's a ripple effect, like a stone being tossed into a pond reverberating outward, creating a network of connections that extend far beyond my own existence. The work I now do in the world has taken moments of struggle and turned them into momentum to continue serving those I am meant to serve.

It is humbling to witness the transformative power of our words and stories shared from our hearts. The more I expose my vulnerabilities and embrace the scars along the way, the more they serve as catalysts for change in the lives of others. The sparks of inspiration that have been ignited, have kindled the flames within others ... with resilience, courage and confidence.

The Journey of Rediscovering My Voice: From Loss to Purposeful Inspiration

Back in 2013, when I lost my voice and life took an unexpected turn that shook me to my core, it seemed like a cruel twist of fate. My voice, both figuratively and literally, had been stripped away. The health ailment that silenced my vocal cords left me with a level of pain I had never known and an inability to communicate in the most fundamental way. Being thrust into a world of isolation, where even the simplest thing like answering a phone was not possible, would bring valuable lessons that I would later learn.

For several years now, I have felt a stronger sense of purpose than ever before. It's as if the stars aligned to guide me toward a path I was destined to tread, and the Universe urged me to embark on an inner journey, a voyage of self-discovery that extended far beyond the limitations of my vocal cords. This journey, along with all its twists, turns and moments of introspection, has transformed me from feeling lost to having a purpose-driven life. What's more, is that it's a journey that wouldn't have been possible without the paradoxical loss and rediscovery of my own voice. My journey may not be exactly like yours; however, it is a reminder that finding meaning in your life is not confined to, nor defined by a particular phase, as we are always evolving.

The journey of finding your purpose is intricately entwined with discovering your authentic voice. Just like that compass that relies on its needle to point the way, your voice guides you toward your purpose. My experience serves as a testament to the transformative power of embracing vulnerability, cultivating resilience, and daring to uncover the voice that has always been within. As you embark upon your own expedition of self-discovery, remember that your voice is not just a tool of expression, it's your own GPS system. Use it as a roadmap that leads you to finding your voice and your purpose in life.

Reflections

- What aspects of your life make you feel most authentic and alive?

- How have previous challenges influenced the way you currently express yourself?

- Recall a moment when you felt a deep sense of resonance with your purpose.

- List three ways you can begin to cultivate resilience in the face of fear and doubt.

- Envision how you want to live your life and express your voice. Start to become that person.

Believe in Yourself: Change Your Mind, Change Your Life

Know that every moment is an opportunity to invite change. You can train and change your mind the moment you decide to start believing in yourself. Don't wait for a new year to make a resolution or that "perfect moment" to start a project or launch your new idea. Just start. Fear of failure is fear of the judgment that your mind tricks you into believing people will think of you if it doesn't work out. Well, what if it does? What if the thing that is holding you back is the very thing that will propel you forward? Your tribe, your people, they will not abandon you. You can do anything you set your mind to. Surround yourself with those who will be there to cheer you on and support you unconditionally. They are the ones who will keep you on the path to finding your purpose and finding your voice.

Renee Reisch

Renee Reisch is a force to be reckoned with in the realm of inspiration and personal growth. With over a decade of experience cultivating and inspiring individuals and teams, her energy is undeniable.

Renee is a Four Times #1 Best-Selling Author, the visionary Founder of Finding Your Voice Network and magazine, and a trusted Women's Life and Leadership Coach. Her unwavering passion lies in assisting women who struggle with self-worth, their voices silenced and their potential untapped. She firmly believes that each individual possesses the power to cultivate steadfast confidence. Through her transformative coaching program, she guides them to unlock their hidden potential.

Renee's life took a dramatic turn when she faced a devastating illness that robbed her of her voice. Several years later, she also experienced the profound loss of her best friend and father. Rather than giving in, she drew inspiration from their example to Never Give Up. That legacy now guides Renee in her own life and in her efforts to serve others.

Connect with Renee at http://www.reneereisch.com.

CHAPTER 17

Let's Do a Cannonball Together!

Sherri Leopold

Dear Emma Leopold and Ivy Sullivan, my beloved granddaughters: I hope you will always embrace and love yourselves completely, radiate your unique light, and live each day with intention and meaning. Please know that you are an unrepeatable miracle! Nana loves you both dearly!

I've been walking towards my purpose most of my life. It became extremely apparent through an experience I had with a friend. My friend was going through a rough time. She asked if she could come over to talk. We started talking about what was happening in her life. She was sitting on my living room floor. There was a moment of quiet when I was looking at her and she just expelled a heavy sigh and shook her head. I said, "Why did you say that to yourself?" She said with a startled look "I didn't say anything!" I responded with, "Oh, you didn't just say to yourself you would always be broke, you'd always be alone, and that you would be stuck in a crappy job forever?" Complete shock registered on her face. I said, "Did you think you needed to say it out loud for me to hear it?"

She didn't. Her self-loathing was written all over her face. Interestingly, she said "WOW!" I suggested we go for a walk and get rid of some of the heavy negative energy that had landed on us. We both felt better after the walk.

Fast forward to the following day, I was on my way to a local networking group. I was listening to the radio and the host came on and announced that Anthony Bourdain had committed suicide just three days after Kate Spade had done the same. OH MY GOD! This has to stop! I didn't realize I literally called God to the car with me. I turned down the radio and started talking to Him out loud. I felt so upset about this even though I didn't know either one of them. As tears stung my eyes, I saw my friend's face as she sat on my floor the night before. She had none of the things they had; no money, no prestige, no fame or hordes of people who loved them, no fabulous job. They had their dream careers, families who loved them, and loads of friends, and my friend didn't have any of that. WHAT was going to keep her from choosing the same end? I felt a rising panic, and an insistent urge to do something. (I was still talking completely out loud to myself in the car driving down the interstate, and I imagine I looked ridiculous.) Because I share vitamins for a living, I had no idea what I could do to help this situation.

Ironically, I had just turned in the final draft of my first collaborative chapter that week, so the first thing to drop in my mind was to write a book. I had a sense of rightness when I said it. That helped me feel like I was on the right track. I continued to talk out loud to myself and I asked myself the question: What do Kate Spade, Anthony Bourdain, and my friend have in common?

What would the common denominator be between the three of them? I needed to know because I did NOT want her to make that same choice.

Then the thought occurred to me. It's what they say to themselves. Self-Bullying. I heard those words so loudly, it was as if they came from the empty seat next to me. I spoke the title out loud at that moment. Self-Bullying: What to do when the bully is you! I felt very excited. This was it. This was what I was supposed to do. I was going to write a book about Self-Bullying. I had no idea exactly how this book would be structured or how it would even come to be, but I felt a calmness come over me. It felt like an affirmation that I was on the right track.

As the months rolled on, I continued to develop the concept, lay out the outline, then wrote the book, and started finding speaking engagements to talk about self-bullying. I call myself the leader of the Stop Self-Bullying Movement. It is a movement because I've made it one. It's part of my mission and my purpose to help all people Stand UP and Stand OUT as the unrepeatable miracle that they are. It took exactly one full year to get to the publish date. Even as this current book is coming to fruition, I am in the process of rewriting a second edition of my Self-Bullying book with all of the knowledge that I have accumulated in the past few years. It's time for an update, and to encourage people to continue in this journey of understanding their worth. WOW is a word I heard repeatedly before I even released the book just based on the title. I incorporated it right into the movement. W.O.W. WARRIOR means Warrior or Woman of Worth Warrior. Ultimately, it refers to someone who knows their value and self-worth, and when they walk in a room, all you can say is WOW!

The Stop Self-Bullying Movement is part of everything I do today. As I stand in my purpose of helping every person Stand UP and Stand OUT as that repeatable miracle, the principles from the book are part of everything I do.

Marie Kondo talks about keeping items and things that spark joy. I believe your purpose should do the same for you. It should spark joy for you every time you stand in it fully. I get to do that now every day through the WOW WARRIOR platform that I created. Today I have created an entire platform that allows people who know their worth, believe in themselves, and know beyond a shadow of a doubt they are here, to serve in a huge way. With the three television shows that I have, I can interview incredible human beings who are making a difference in the world simply by being themselves. They have the confidence to stand in their purpose and build their legacies, and I have the honor to be part of it. I also use the WOW WARRIOR magazine as a platform for people to share their expertise and showcase their incredible talents. They can Stand UP and Stand OUT as the unrepeatable miracle that they are inside those pages, and shine as the great humans they are. Seeing others succeed is truly what sparks joy for me. It is wrapped up in my purpose.

I'm often heard saying that my purpose is completely tied to yours. By that, I mean that if I help you expand your visibility and help you grow, I'm fulfilling my purpose. This came in some moments of clarity during the pandemic. During that time, we had a lot of time to think and do some introspection. I took advantage of that time to figure out what I wanted to be known for. It was really about Legacy for me. In 2023, my word for the year is Legacy. For me, Legacy is tied tightly to the word purpose, because your purpose, and standing in your purpose, is what creates your legacy. I took many long walks during the pandemic, which gave me the time and environment to help me understand myself at a level I wouldn't otherwise have. What became very clear to me was that life is all about choices. I am famous for the phrase:

Choices create change; change your choices and your choices change.

Many of us want to stay stuck in the same old routine, and we avoid change. However, change is the only constant we truly have. I might be weird in the fact that I truly love change. When things are always exactly the same, that is what makes me feel uncomfortable.

As I have walked along this journey, I have helped many people along the way. One of those people was my friend, who sat on my floor at the beginning of this chapter. I have had the honor and pleasure of mentoring her and watching her adapt to and embrace change. She has decided to live life a different way. She is growing, and because she has made different choices, her choices have changed. She has improved her job situation, changed her relationships, and quadrupled her confidence level by learning to walk in her own purpose. She has up-leveled her income and is so much happier overall. She regularly thanks me for mentoring and encouraging her. It has been extraordinary to be part of her journey and has reaffirmed that my journey is tied to others' journeys. I am most fulfilled when I am helping someone else walk in their purpose. That is a big part of my purpose.

Another person who comes to mind is a gentleman that I met on an airplane. It's a great story in that we were both headed to Las Vegas and were not supposed to be sitting next to each other. A mother with three children traveling alone (including an infant) was sitting in the other two seats next to his and their other seat was the one that was next to me on the other side of the aisle. She asked him if he would mind moving to the other seat so she could sit with her children and he was immediately out of his seat and heading across the aisle. He was relieved to be sitting next to me instead of three children under the age of six. I looked at him and thought maybe he was from another country. He didn't say much, but I did notice he was reading a book that was a business building book. I struck up a conversation with him because I had not read that book, and I asked him about it. We began to chat and I asked him what he was doing while in Las Vegas, then about what business he was in. He was very friendly, and we exchanged contact information. I checked in with him while he was in Vegas, and we continued to talk after the trip, then began doing some business together. What seemed so random was so meant to be. In our five years of knowing one another, I have mentored him in building a successful business and helping people in the disability community. He has also created a lifestyle magazine for the disability community called Imagine the World (IWO) As One. I have watched and encouraged his growth. His confidence, and leadership abilities have increased in a way that could only be described as magnificent. I've seen him attract an amazing life partner, nurture his successful magazine, and continue to teach children in special education. His personal growth has been incredible. Seeing this growth gives me joy. He calls me Mentor Mom, which makes me proud and gives me a giggle.

If I have a day where I feel like I'm falling short, I think of these two friends and know that someone is waiting for me to show up and create a ripple of blessings with them. It brings to mind what Danelle Delgado always teaches in her training. Who loses if I don't win? If I don't show up and impact—who misses out? It makes me refocus and keep going. Someone is waiting for me, even when I don't know it.

If I gave a visual of my purpose it would be this; Imagine running off the end of a dock and doing a cannonball into a lake. You'd certainly make a splash. My goal and purpose is to run off that dock WITH you at full speed and do a cannonball, arm and arm because together, we can make a much bigger splash and create a bigger ripple of blessings to others!

When I interview someone, share an article they wrote, or promote something for them, this is me running off the dock with them—doing a giant cannonball with them! Be prepared! I'll be laughing, yelling, and cheering the whole way down the dock!

One of the inherent challenges I face in helping people Stand UP and Stand OUT by running and jumping off that dock is that sometimes I feel like I shouldn't charge for it. I have to routinely remind myself that it takes time and money to promote, edit, and share what someone else is doing. Even though I love doing it, I still need to be compensated for it. If I do it for free, I devalue myself but I devalue the customer as well. They will not value my time or the interview when they don't pay for it. I believe the saying is:

Those who pay, pay attention!

I also know that paying for interviews or articles that require my time is respecting my self-worth. My time is also valuable. I AM VALUABLE. I remind myself this is how I personally Stand UP and Stand OUT.

There have been many times that I didn't know if I should continue with something related to my purpose because I wasn't making enough money from it. I have concluded that when things are done with your purpose in mind, it isn't all about the money. It is also about the impact! I will always prioritize impact over income. I don't plan on taking any money with me, but I do plan on leaving a legacy behind with the people I have served.

I want to finish by talking about Legacy. A definition of Legacy is the long-lasting impact of particular events, actions, etc. that you have facilitated by finding your purpose.

This reflects back to the quote:

Choices create change. Change your choices and your choices change.

I made choices intentionally to create the change I wanted. I designed a life that I am happy to say I lived fully and loved every minute of it, even the hard parts! I created a magazine and three interview shows because I wanted to.

Each time something was hard. I made a choice, even if it was difficult. Inaction is a choice. Inaction is not for me. Finding your purpose is about finding a way to have the impact you want to have, no matter what it takes to do it. It's your choice between becoming a WOW Warrior or sitting back on the sidelines and seeing what happens. It is the difference between reacting and responding. Inaction only allows space to react. Action allows you to stand in your power and respond, instead of someone or something dictating your reaction.

I encourage you to execute your power of choice! Your choices will create the legacy you can leave. It will pave the road in your journey with joyful experiences, gratitude-filled moments, and true fulfillment.

I encourage you to Stand UP and Stand OUT as the unrepeatable miracle you are and know that there is NO ONE like you.

YOU are an unrepeatable miracle!

Find your purpose and go do big things!

Sherri Leopold

Sherri Leopold is an exceptional leader who has dedicated her life to empowering people and promoting self-love. As the CEO of Option Creators Inc., she is a mentor, speaker, and the Leader of the Stop Self-Bullying Movement. Through her WOW WARRIOR platform, she has created a space for women to connect, support each other, and celebrate their worth. Sherri is also a magazine publisher, interview show host and 10-time bestselling author. Her shows, including WOW WARRIOR, WOW- Look Who's Here, and Outside the Box with Sherri Leopold, reach audiences across social media channels and through Everydaywomantv.com. With over 30 years of experience in speaking, mentoring, and team building, Sherri is a valuable resource for personal growth and financial success. As a State Director and Chancellor Mentor with Givers University, she is committed to helping others transform their lives both mentally and physically through being a true giver.

Connect with Sherri at https://sherrileopold.com/.

CHAPTER 18

Rediscovering A New Purpose

Teresa Dawn Johnson

I dedicate my chapter to my sons, Sean and Nicholas, who
both taught me to be the parent I needed to be and for
making me a better person.

When I was in junior high, I discovered a love for interviewing students and teachers for our school newspaper. I enjoyed my journalism class so much that I had intentions of going to college to major in journalism. I envisioned my purpose as more of my career goals than I did my purpose. Shortly after graduating college, I started my career at a small newspaper. Then I met my sons' father. We soon started a family.

At nine months, my oldest son, Sean, started showing developmental delays. He could not bear any weight on his legs and he could not sit up independently. His father and I took him to be seen by the doctor and he recommended physical therapy and speech therapy. At the time, the health insurance companies were not paying for speech therapy, so we were able to get help through Easter Seals. Easter Seals provides services to ensure that children with developmental delays, disabilities, and other special needs can reach their full potential. Sean was enrolled in speech therapy, physical therapy, and occupational therapy until he started preschool where he would continue to receive the same services.

While Sean was receiving speech therapy at Taylorville Memorial Hospital, his speech therapist asked me what I did during the day. I let her know I was a stay-at-home mom with Sean. She said that Easter Seals needed help and asked if I would be willing to accept donations from businesses and speak to civic organizations about Easter Seals. Back then, I was timid to speak in front of groups, but as a mom desperate to get the help my son needed, I volunteered to help with Easter Seals. I would speak about what Easter Seals did as an organization and how the valuable speech therapy helped my son and other children.

By the time Sean was two, he was diagnosed with autism. Around the time Sean was nine years old, I was introduced to an autism parent support group, in Springfield, Illinois: Autism Society of America Central Illinois Chapter. I felt heard and included during the support group meetings. The other parents who served on the board of directors wanted me to serve on the board. With my writing skills and genuine care for others, they saw me as an asset to the group. With another board member, I co-produced the group's newsletter. I helped with our annual golf outing fundraiser.

There was an opportunity for our group to send a board member to a weekend leadership retreat. At the retreat, I learned that in order for our group to be a success, it would be best for us not to rely on one main fundraiser. Our board brainstormed on an idea to have an autism awareness walk. We formed a committee to plan the autism awareness walk. I would assist with promoting on local television and radio stations, as well as, help the committee with other duties. Until our board was able to hire a part-time office person, we had a voicemail system that would record voicemail to text via email to all the board members. I would get these emails as soon as they appeared and I was usually the first one to call the parents back. I soon realized I enjoyed helping other parents find the resources they were looking for. I remembered how it was for our family when we were looking for help. I knew what it was like for the parents needing help. I served on the autism parent board for six years. My youngest son wanted me to be more available to him, especially on the one night a month we had our board meeting. The meetings tended to get long and I then had a thirty-minute drive home.

During the time I spent with the autism support group, I found my purpose. I did not go looking for my purpose. My purpose found me. I feel warm and accepted when I am helping others. I believe we are here to serve others. The group gave to me and I also wanted to give back.

For we are God's handiwork, created in Christ Jesus to do good works, which God prepared in advance for us to do.
~Ephesians 2:10

After I departed from the autism group, I remained connected to the other parents. I also became more connected to our local group of young adults with Special Olympics, called Kids Are Kids. Sean enjoyed bowling and basketball skills competitions. The Kids Are Kids group also holds dances once a month.

There are seven things I learned being a mom and a caregiver for Sean and as a mom to his younger brother, Nick.

I learned to be an advocate. An advocate is someone who supports or recommends a particular cause or policy. I advocate for both of my sons in their education. Since Sean was a special education student, he had an individual education program, IEP, that the school produced and implemented. In the first few annual IEP meetings, I did not know what I was doing. I did not understand the reports the therapists and teachers were giving. Thankfully, with my involvement with the autism parent group, we had an IEP coach who walked us through how to advocate for our children. My youngest son, Nick, was having trouble focusing and losing his completed homework. I worked with his school to get a plan in place to have his teacher look at his written assignments and have time to clean out his locker during study hall. As an adult, Nick now knows how to advocate for himself, which brings me great joy.

I learned to have empathy for others. In going through the challenges of not having a break or respite in caring for Sean full time, I easily understood what other parents go through. The care involved in taking care of a child or adult with special needs is difficult. I understand the needs of other families are tremendous and not just for my own family.

I learned patience. I know before becoming a parent, I had no patience. I wanted everything now and I disliked waiting. Sean, due to his autism, had some mood swings. Sometimes he would get overwhelmed, sad, or angry. I knew he did not know how to regulate his emotions. Unfortunately, by the later years in his teens, he had to be on medication to help his emotions, because he would sometimes hurt himself or hit the wall. It would sometimes benefit Sean if I came beside him and rubbed his back or hugged him. It would take him a while to calm his emotions and this taught me to be patient. It would be calm in his time, not mine.

I learned kindness. I learned to be kind to others through my own experience. I had a lot of rough days as a parent. I knew other parents were also having rough days, especially parents of those with special needs.

I learned gratitude. I grew up in a household where a lot of time was spent looking at negative things and what was going wrong. I learned to start thinking of what was going right and that perspective is gratitude and to look at things to be thankful for. Many days were difficult being a parent and caregiver, but if we got through the day without a meltdown, I could focus on the gratitude of not having a meltdown. One time at a store, Sean did have a meltdown. I was trying to be patient and get through the checkout as quickly as I could. Sean continued to be upset all the way out to the car in the parking lot. A man came up to me in the parking lot and asked me if I was okay. I was not, but was a little better knowing there was someone who asked about my well-being and who cared. That day, I focused on the gratitude that Sean and I had made it out of the store and that another person shared such kindness.

I learned self-care. When my youngest son, Nick, was two years old, I was invited to a gathering where I was to bring two to three photos. We were going to learn about taking care of photographs and archiving them in albums so they would not get damaged by sticky pages, acid, and lignin. I would also learn scrapbooking would be a great hobby that would get me away from the house and get a break from my kids. Parents, and especially special needs parents, need a break so they can recharge. Getting a self-care boost allows us to come back to caring for our loved ones in a better way. We come back feeling new energy and continue to care for and love our loved ones without feeling tired and sometimes resentful.

I learned to help others. Giving our time, patience, compassion, and love is the highest form of service there is.

For those searching for your purpose, I would recommend not looking too hard. Likely, your skills or the people that you surround yourself with will nudge your purpose out. I know that whatever my purpose looks like, it will involve helping others.

In March 2023, my oldest son, Sean, passed unexpectedly. I had not realized until his passing how much my identity was in being my son's caretaker. I spent every morning through the work week getting him ready to go to his day program, while I got myself ready for work. Then, after I got home from work, I took care of my son, got the evening meal done, and then got Sean ready for bed. He had the cognitive ability of a five-year-old, although he passed just two weeks before his twenty-eighth birthday.

I am attempting to find my new normal, my new routine, my new purpose. I am rediscovering who I am. My purpose has shifted. I am on a new path. I am looking for my new life purpose, but in that one element that I am seeking, I have the need and the opportunity to help others. I will use my life experience to help others.

I also recommend, when searching for your purpose, talking to God. I have. Okay, Lord, You have brought me to this point in my life. What do you have for me next? I am willing to let God work through me to help others. I am asking for God's guidance in *Rediscovering a New Purpose*.

Teresa D. Johnson

Teresa D. Johnson is an insurance professional, a blogger, author, and entrepreneur who resides in Taylorville, Illinois. Johnson was born in central Illinois and lived in Florida and Texas for a short time when she was young. It was during her time in Texas that she discovered her talent for writing and won first place in a statewide academic essay competition at the University of Texas in 1982. She later graduated with a Bachelor of Arts degree in journalism and political science. She freelanced for the Springfield Business Journal, a monthly business publication from the fall of 2001 to January 2016.

Teresa is an anti-bully advocate supporting Stand for the Silent and a former six-year parent board member of the Autism Society of America Central Illinois Chapter. Teresa is a single parent and has advocated for both her sons: Sean and Nick. She advocated not only for autism but ADHD in relation to her youngest son, Nick. With encouragement from her youngest son, she sought an ADHD evaluation in November 2022 and was diagnosed with ADHD, in December 2022.

Teresa has a passion for advocating for individuals with autism and their families by providing knowledge to access community services and financial solutions to help bring peace to the entire family.

Connect with Teresa at https://linktr.ee/officialtimewithteresa.

CHAPTER 19

The Ultimate Success Metric

Terry Shepherd

To Colleen. None of this would have happened without you.

The Ultimate Success Metric may not be what we think it is.

I moved back to Michigan for a second appearance in 2010. I knew the lay of the land well and swung out of the city toward a strip mall barbershop I remembered from 1976, when I was working my way through college as a screaming top-40 DJ. The place was still there and had the lived-in look of a business stewarded by a half dozen owners. By now, I was a relatively known quantity in town and was used to being known. I saw the man behind the barber chair nod, a half-smile of recognition cleaving dimples into his features.

About halfway through the haircut, he asked, "Are you the same guy I used to listen to on the radio when I was in junior high?" I admitted it.

From somewhere behind a row of clippers and hair tonics, he produced an American Graffiti album. "You signed this for me at a dance."

Here's how the universe works. At that moment, his wife appeared in the doorway. He introduced us and she asked for my phone number. It brought back memories of my single days when that question was a buying sign. But this was different. She called later that night to share how my newfound barber had a challenging adolescence. "Your show was the one thing that got him through it."

I continued to patronize his shop. As our friendship deepened, I learned that he had always wanted to be a teacher. His father insisted he enter the family business. For twenty years, he spent his days accepting fate and wishing he could be somewhere else.

Time passed. Between us, his wife and I convinced him to go for the college degree he always wanted. He followed my path into broadcasting, still wishing he could pass on his knowledge to a new generation of kids who might have shared his struggles.

Then came Covid. Classroom teachers started to fall away from the profession and the state gave guys, like my barber, the chance to show their stuff without the once-required teaching certificate. As I write this, he's in his second year as a middle school shop teacher, loving life as never before and inspiring young people to dream beyond their self-imposed limitations.

His wife traces it all back to those late nights in the '70s when I was spinning "Blinded By the Light," and affirming the self-esteem of an invisible audience, just as my own radio mentors did *when I was his age*.

Each of us keeps a personal scorecard with which we judge ourselves and those around us. We measure everything from financial wealth to educational attainment, from athletic achievement to career progression. We inventory material possessions and paint happy pictures of our lives on social media to show others how successful we are.

Are we measuring the right things?

We all know unhappy rich people, highly educated individuals who are incapable of interpersonal relationships and former elite athletes who struggle with life after they can no longer keep up on the playing field. We've also attended class reunions where someone we least expected to achieve has found a fulfilling career with rewards that extend well beyond monetary compensation.

Without realizing it, during those days on the radio in 1976, I had made a difference for at least one of my listeners.

If I had to pick just one metric to define a life well lived, it would be this:

The most important indicator of a successful human existence is the extent to which we can positively impact the lives of others.

Hold this standard against the exploits, good and bad, that are chronicled in our newscasts. How many of them qualify?

How many of the actions of the politicians we have elected to represent us pass the Ultimate Success Metric test?

Now, let's look in the mirror. How much of the time and energy you have invested during this past week was directed toward this ideal?

If positively impacting the lives of others was a daily test, how often would you pass, or fail?

The Ultimate Success Metric is tied to an underlying concept that is the foundation for all meaningful achievement: Purpose.

In the grand tapestry of life, finding and pursuing purpose is a transformative journey that can bring fulfillment, meaning and direction. Yet, the concept of purpose can often seem elusive and overwhelming.

Purpose is the guiding force that propels us forward, giving our lives depth, significance and a sense of direction. It is the reason we wake up each day with a sense of anticipation and motivation. Purpose provides us with clarity and helps us understand our unique role in the world. It goes beyond external achievements and delves into the realm of inner fulfillment, aligning our actions with our values and passions.

Purpose answers life's key question: What were we put here to do? The world's greatest thinkers have pondered this, distilling it into eight magic words that fit every situation.

Our purpose in life is to alleviate suffering.

We are rewarded for helping others solve their problems. For alleviating their pain. For helping them find their own path purpose and positioning their passions and skill sets to chase it.

Living a purposeful life requires embracing integrity, authenticity and a commitment to living in harmony with our beliefs. When our actions reflect our values, we experience a deep sense of congruence and fulfillment. This alignment empowers us to make choices that are in line with our purpose, paving the way for personal growth and positive impact.

Purpose evolves and expands as we grow and learn. Embracing growth means being open to new experiences, challenges and opportunities for self-discovery. It involves taking calculated risks, stepping out of comfort zones and embracing change. Recognizing that our purpose may evolve over time allows us to remain flexible and adaptable, unlocking new layers of meaning and fulfillment along our journey.

Pursuing purpose is inextricably tied to <u>The Ultimate Metric</u>. It means using our unique talents, resources, and passions to make a difference in the lives of those around us. Whether it's through acts of kindness, mentorship, or contributing to a cause, we have the power to create a ripple effect of positive change. Leaving a lasting legacy is the culmination of a purposeful life, ensuring that our impact continues beyond our lifetime.

How do we pursue purpose while living in *the now?*

The journey begins with an assessment of what activities or causes bring us joy, enthusiasm and a sense of fulfillment. Reflecting on our natural talents, interests and values can help us identify the areas that resonate deeply within our souls. Whether it's creativity, helping others, or pursuing knowledge, our passions are key indicators that guide us towards a purposeful path.

Assessing the skills we bring to the table is essential. We each come into the world with a toolbox. Through education and experience, we add tools to that collection. Aligning our gifts with a purposeful passion can help power us through every obstacle, keep the faith when the rain comes and stay humble when inevitable achievement finds us.

When I was just starting out on the radio, a guy I admired told me I would never make it. "You've got a tenor voice and a speech impediment. Forget that dream."

Yeah, that one hurt. But something strange happened. I channeled all the pain and disappointment into energy. I decided I would become one of the best broadcasting practitioners ever. My detractor was right. There was a steep uphill climb. I endured multiple rejections and setbacks. The one thing that didn't change was my focus. And as we all know, our focus determines our direction.

With patient practice, I improved. I began to sound more like the role models I revered. I climbed the professional ladder, ultimately earning the opportunity to ply my trade on the very Detroit radio station that first stirred my passion.

I also learned that performing on air was neither my full-time passion nor purpose. Goals have a way of morphing with experience and wisdom. In the ensuing years, I never totally left my first love behind. Along the way, I was lucky to paint audio tapestries across a plethora of commercials, documentaries and movie trailers. Today, I own the radio station brand that first fired my enthusiasm and inspired me to dream beyond the horizon.

If I had not followed that path, my barber might still be cutting hair. I would never have met my beloved wife of 45 years. And the grandchildren I chase around the yard, would be in someone else's cosmos.

The purpose of life is not to be happy. It is to be useful, to be honorable, to be compassionate, to have it make some difference that you have lived and lived well.
~Ralph Waldo Emerson

William Arthur Ward created some of the 20th century's most quoted maxims. He puts it this way:

Do more than belong: participate. Do more than care: help. Do more than believe: practice. Do more than be fair: be kind. Do more than dream: work.
~ William Arthur Ward

The commonalities all people we define as successful share is a work ethic. Your contacts, your parents, perhaps your money may open doors. You won't be allowed to stay without earning it every day.

Zig Ziglar, the legendary motivational speaker told me he gave over 10,000 speeches for free before he earned his first paycheck in the trade. Paul McCartney can't read a note of music and is self-taught on guitar, drums, and piano ... left-handed. The Beatles toiled in German bars, perfecting their trademark vibe over several years, honing their act and building the creative partnership that would change our musical canon forever.

In both cases, the vision was clear, and the pursuit was inexorable.

Not everyone is capable of goodness. Evil exists in our world. Neutralizing evil liberates those whom it afflicts. For this reason, we are grateful for the men and women who willingly put their lives on the line to protect us.

You attack to protect, not to avenge. You strike to end
suffering, not cause it.
~Tiana Dalichov in her novel *Agenda 46*

I've always been an advocate for women and the disaffected. I've forgotten how many times my bosses warned me, "Are you willing to risk your career for that person?" If the individual had the goods, I rolled the dice.

It didn't always work. Some of my most painful moments resulted from helping someone who took advantage of my kindness and then turned on me. During one of the darkest moments of my professional life, my father reminded me, "Our lives are a body of work, not a single incident. Keep doing good things." Those turned out to be his last words. I've never forgotten them.

Evil only wins if you allow it to distract you from The Ultimate Success Metric.

Here's one of my favorite quotes. It clearly articulates both the *what* and the *how* of the Ultimate Success Metric:

All labor that uplifts humanity has dignity and importance and should be undertaken with painstaking excellence.
~Dr. Martin Luther King, Jr.

To what extent can you invest *painstaking excellence* to positively impact the lives of others?

There is only one comportment you need to bring to this task: Model the behaviors you expect, every day, everywhere. You may not do it well in the beginning. Some days may feel like you've taken one step forward and two steps backward. But like all skills, yours will improve with practice.

My barber friend, now a beloved classroom teacher knew the secret. "I didn't have good role models in my family," he told me. "So, I found my own."

We are given two families by the universe: The biological family who gave us life and the wide portfolio of people we choose to fill in the blanks. My high school English teacher opened my eyes to writing fiction, when he introduced us to Ray Bradbury's *Rocket Man* by way of Elton John. My second Jessica Ramirez thriller, *Chasing the Captain* is dedicated to his memory. One of my father's friends sent me Robert Greenleaf's seminal writing on *Servant Leadership*. We had amazing conversations on the topic for the rest of his life, and my ability to lead with compassion improved.

In every endeavor, I've sought out the smartest and most thoughtful people I could find who had already mastered that which I hoped to learn. It was the same story when I began my writer's journey. Dan Brown, Megan Abbott, James Paterson and Allison Leotta were the first four people I approached for advice. I was pleasantly surprised, when each went above and beyond my one question to help me learn **the Craft**.

Their only request: Pass it on ...

One of the best books ever written about networking is Keith Ferrazzi's, *Never Eat Alone*. I've interviewed Keith. Yup, I identified him as one of the best of the best in that space and found a way to spend time with him. He posits that there are some 200 people who will determine the extent of our achievements in life. We need to identify them and learn from them. But first, we must find a way to add value to their endeavors. Keith told me, "The only way to get an exponential payback is to authentically give without the expectation of return."

When I work with authors on promoting their books and their brand, I suggest that they approach the organizations and individuals who can help them with service on their minds. How do these people define purpose and passion? What things can the authors do to open doors and ease their journey in the direction of their dreams? Shotgun email requests and cold calls without knowing another person's world often end unproductively.

Earl Nightingale, the renowned success philosopher, tells the story of a man who was searching for a job during the great depression. In a time when millions were out of work and many companies were on the brink of bankruptcy, the man approached his search in a unique way.

First, he decided what he wanted to do. He had the same purpose, passion, talent conversation we are having now. Then he studied the organizations that were most closely aligned with his ethics and objectives. He did his homework on their products, services, and competitors, how they created value and earned income, and the huge obstacles the depression put in their way.

When he had studied and thought about it all, he made an appointment to see the head of the company where he wanted to work. This was his pitch.

"I've been thinking about the challenges your firm is facing and I have several ideas to share with you about how to overcome them."

With so many competitors begging for a job from a CEO who was, himself, a single thread away from disaster, here was one person who came with ideas and energy to help solve his problems.

The applicant got the job. Earl added a postscript. The man rose steadily through the ranks, ultimately earning the exact position he had focused on.

What is our take-away from this story? Another Zig Ziglar gem:

Help people get what they need and you
will get what you need.
~Zig Ziglar

Or as Earl often said,

Our rewards in life are in exact proportion to our
contributions, our service.
~Earl Nightingale

Our little publishing company helps independent authors navigate taking their stories from ideas to the printed page. We have forged strong working relationships with exceptional editors, cover designers, public relations professionals, and audio book narrators. What started out as an entity to pass the copyrights of my own books on to my children has grown into a community of purpose and passion; people who help one another achieve their objectives.

The other day, I found myself sitting next to my client, the gifted author, Laura Kemp, at a small farmers' market in rural Michigan. I helped replenish her stock as customers made their purchases. And I watched her interactions. Sales were made when readers discerned that the stories she tells could give them an escape from an uncertain world. She was alleviating suffering by transporting people into a world where romance and the paranormal intersect. The dozens of five-star Amazon reviews confirmed it. In between the produce and trinkets that drew people to the market, she offered transport to another world. We both felt great whenever a customer walked away with one of her books under their arm, secure in the knowledge that she was adding value, making someone else's life a little better, living at the intersection of purpose, passion and talent, and loving it.

Keep the Ultimate Success Metric at the front of your mind. Once the purpose is clear, the metric will clarify, too.

When you dedicate your life to positively impacting the lives of others, no obstacle will stop you from pursuing your quest. The Ultimate Success Metric is the only score that really matters. There is no greater need and no higher calling.

Terry Shepherd

Terry Shepherd is the author of the Jessica Ramirez Thrillers, The 221B Club stories for mid-grade readers and the Covid-19 children's classic, Juliette and the Mystery Bug. Terry's short stories have been published in several anthologies. He is also a prolific book narrator and owns a publishing company focused on helping indie authors get their stories into wide circulation. He lives and writes on the ocean in Jacksonville, Florida.

Connect with Terry at https://terryshepherd.com/.

AFTERWORD

It is our sincere hope that these stories have not only caused you to think, but to ACT! As you have read through the chapters, you have seen the authors experience many challenges on their journeys to finding their purpose. You probably also noticed they made a decision to uplevel their lives.

Some stories highlighted mental or emotional health or wellness, and some physical or spiritual wellness and, yet others, financial wellness. The common thread through all of our stories is that we chose not to stay stuck in a state of unwellness or unhappiness, but to persevere through it all.

May today be the day you are inspired to choose to create the life you deserve, be courageous enough to act, and surround yourself with winners who want you to win as well.

Today is the perfect day to Take Action!

If any of these stories resonated with you, please connect with the author. They are here to help you Find Your Purpose.

Lynda Sunshine West and Sally Larkin Green

READER BONUS!

Dear Reader,

As a thank you for your support, Action Takers Publishing would like to offer you a special reader bonus: a free download of our course, "How to Write, Publish, Market & Monetize Your Book the Fast, Fun & Easy Way." This comprehensive course is designed to provide you with the tools and knowledge you need to bring your book to life and turn it into a successful venture.

The course typically **retails for $499**, but as a valued reader, you can access it for free. To claim your free download, simply follow this link ActionTakersPublishing.com/workshops - use the discount code "coursefree" to get a 100% discount and start writing your book today.

If we are still giving away this course by the time you're reading this book, head straight over to your computer and start the course now. It's absolutely free.

READER BONUS!

ActionTakersPublishing.com/workshops
discount code "coursefree"

Made in United States
Orlando, FL
22 December 2023